3 Years

3 Years

Healing Not Healed

Chavanese Wint

Published by Icons Media Publishing in 2024

Copyright © Chavanese Wint

First Edition

The author asserts the moral right under the Copyright, Designs and Patents Act 1988 to be identified as the author of this work.

All Rights reserved. No part of this publication may be reproduced, stored in a retrieval system or transmitted, in any form or by any means without the prior consent of the author, nor be otherwise circulated in any form of binding or cover other than that in which it is published and without a similar condition being imposed on the subsequent purchaser.

Contents

Writer's Resurgence 1
Ink & Reflections 3
The Unwritten Manual 5
One Step at a Time 6
In the Shadows of Mortality 7
In the Arms of the Breeze 9
Love's Serendipity 11
The Final Reckoning 13
Mindful Retreat 15
Sunday's Deadly Curse 17
The Weight Debate 19
Embracing Arborophilia 21
Life 23
The Unseen Impact 24
The Unexpected Goodbye 26
Rise and Thrive 27
The Mighty Pen 29
Preserving the Sacred 31
To Death, We All Owe 32
Lost in the Noise 34
The Journey to Wholeness 35
Invisible Battles 36
The Healing Power of the Gym 37
Despairful Silence 39
Whew Who knew 41
Lessons in Love 42
Love's Souvenirs 43
Unveiling the Reality 45
My Soul's Melody 46

Seeking Answers After Death *47*
From Ashes to Strength *49*
Transcending the Flesh's Finality *50*
Embracing the Journey to Happiness *52*
Chevan *53*
A Poetic Ode to Love and Longing *55*
Mindful Musings *56*
Awakening the Spirit *58*
Purposeful Living *59*
The Dreamer's Manifesto *60*
Washed by Grace *62*
The Illusion of Connection *64*
Toxicity Unmasked *66*
Echoes of Your Absence *68*
The Symphony of My Love *70*
Ethereal Aroma *72*
Time's Captive *74*
Seeking Divine Guidance *75*
The Tapestry of Time *77*
The Human Network *78*
Embodying the Light *80*
Tresses of Transformation *82*
No More Swearing *84*
Love in Different Tongues *86*
Love's Departure *88*
Finding the Balance *90*
The Enchanting World of Swans *92*
The Strength in Softness *94*
When Every Soul Meets Its Boon *96*
Embracing Solitude *98*
Eternal Sisterhood *100*

Rain's Magic...*102*
The Metabolic Disadvantage *104*
Unveiling the Truth..*106*
Awakening the True Self *108*
Mental Fitness...*110*
Building a Resilient Mind *112*
Eternal Wanderer..*114*
The Mirror Within *116*
Journey of the Soul *117*
Ego's Grip...*119*
Embracing the Warrior Within *121*
Unbreakable Mentality *123*
Heaven's Embrace..*125*
Positive Seeds *126*
Personal Paradise...*128*
Life's Ruthless Tempest...*130*
Unburdening the Soul *132*
Love's Symphony *133*
My Unforgotten Soul..*135*
Love Yourself First..*137*
In the Arms of Morpheus...*139*
Beyond Desire *141*
Through a Parent's Eyes *143*
Taking a Digital Detox *145*
Dying in My Dreams...*147*
Your Heavenly Adventure..*149*
Purifying the Mind..*151*
Replacing Love with Aspiration *153*
The Borrowed Time Lifestyle....................................*155*
The Phoenix Effect...*157*
Guardian of the Skies *159*

The Shadows of Memory *161*
Forever in My Heart *163*
Resisting Temptation *165*
Manifesting Miracles *167*
Your Existence Will Cease *169*
Never Settle *171*
The Bitter Taste of Envy *172*
Writing a New Story *174*
A Self-Discovery Through Purposeful Games *176*

DEDICATION

To Shermaine Campbell

Writer's Resurgence

Time: 04:56
Date: 22/11/23

It was hard for me to pick up that pen again,
Strangely enough, it was because of Ben.

~

After the death of a friend,
Who had been with me through thick and thin,
We shared laughter, tears, and everything within.

~

I didn't see it happening, I didn't know when,
It was as if I had emerged from a lion's den.

~

Three years of pain,
Three years of learning,
Three years of understanding oneself,
It felt like a constant yearning.

~

Three years to comprehend my emotions,
Searching for answers in the vast oceans.

~

It took me three years, and now I'm emerging,
Like a phoenix rising from the ashes, my soul urging.

~

Picking up that pen again felt so guilty,
As if my heart was burdened with shame, it almost killed me.

~

But I knew I had to stop the self-pity,
For it was keeping me locked in a state of misery,
I have to remember that even though you're not here,
You will always be with me.

~

As I dipped the pen in ink hesitatingly,
A flood of memories rushed over me.
Words started flowing, forming lines of poetry,
Expressing the depth of my emotions, setting my soul free.

~

Each word felt like a release,
A healing balm for my wounded soul,

A way to make sense of the pain that took its toll.
With every stroke, the pen became my voice,
A conduit for the emotions that were once my choice.
~
The pages filled with verses,
Capturing the essence of a love that never disperses.
~
Each line resonated with the memories we shared,
The moments that proved how much we truly cared.
~
As I penned down the final verse,
A tear escaped, my heart feeling both heavy and rehearsed.
The last word left me hanging, my thoughts suspended,
The story unfinished, and the pain yet not mended.
~
For now, our story remains untold,
Leaving room for imagination to unfold,
A tale that will forever be cherished and never grow old.

Ink & Reflections

Time: 04:56
Date: 28/11/23

Welcome dear reader, to a journey stark,
through a world where longing leaves its mark.

~

Once a vibrant soul, radiant with life's gleam,
Now carries a void, deep and extreme.
A friend, a confidante, both riveting and kind,
Yet she was snatched away, leaving me behind.

~

Her departure, a dagger, piercing through my core,
Each day without her, harder than the one before.
I tread around the globe, my heart in a dreadful reel,
Seeking solace, a remedy that could help me heal.

~

Gone were the days of shared laughter and cheer,
Now replaced with solitude, and echoes of yesteryear.
Ghostly whispers of our past, in every corner they peal,
Reminding me of a wound that time refused to seal.

~

Yet, in the realm of dreams, she comes alive,
Her gaze so profound, it seems to dive,
Right into my soul, stirring memories afresh,
Of a time when we were queens, our spirits meshed.

~

From the silly fights to secret schemes,
Our shared dreams, now lost in time's streams.
Her loss felt like a cruel play of fate's scene,
Could it have been avoided with a simple vaccine?

~

Yet, I try to find solace in this relentless strife,
That death is but a part of everyone's life.
It might have taken her, but could not her essence seize,
Her spirit lingers, a soothing, gentle breeze.

~

So, I stride forth, with a promise made to keep,
In this world, or the next, our reunion will be steep.

At the heavenly gates, with curry goat, rice and peas,
We'll share a meal, as our hearts find their ease.
~
As my tale finds its pause here, in this earthly domain,
A sense of peace, amid the lingering pain.
~
Life and death, paths that intertwined,
Left behind a story, of friendships, love and family undefined.
~
As you close this chapter, you might wonder still,
Was it real? Or a figment of skilled quill?

Truth or fiction, only time can reveal,
Until then, let your imagination take the wheel.

The Unwritten Manual

Time: 02:04
Date: 27/11/23

Life wasn't a tutorial, but a journey to be splendid.
You live, you breathe, then one day you're expended.
They weep, they mourn, to your memorial they attended.

~

Life's not a document where you can etch an edit,
Or a column to revise, or an editorial for credit.
So, I chose to steer my existence, with a spirit entrepreneurial,
Living out my days, making every breath special.

~

When birth ushers you into this grand, cryptic globe,
There's no guidebook, no compass, nor a philosopher's robe.
We strive, we fight, our bodies often bearing the load,
Wound by the whip of time, down an uncertain road.

~

Many gaze upon us, indifferent to our existence.
They care not whether we persist or leave without resistance.
That's when a higher faith steps in, offering assistance,
In God, we trust, drawing strength from His persistence.

~

Life isn't a tutorial, but it's a journey to be learned,
A journey filled with mistakes from which wisdom must be earned.
Chasing the sun's golden trails, the midnight oil is burned,
The pages of our life's book cannot be unturned.

~

We lay our hopes on destiny, on a path divinely lit,
In the face of adversity, never choosing to quit.
With entrepreneurial grace, we make every second count,
In God, we trust, His blessings to surmount.

~

Life is not a tutorial, but a riddle of time,
A dance with destiny, a journey so sublime.

One Step at a Time

Time: 02:20
Date: 28/11/23

I found myself lost,
The weight of guilt consuming me, at any cost.
The world seemed bleak, my heart heavy with pain,
Learning how to smile again seemed an impossible gain.

~

A traumatic experience had shattered my soul,
Leaving me broken, crawling towards a new goal.
Each step outside, a challenge to face,
Counting to ten, preparing for the embrace.

~

Days turned to nights, sleep became my solace,
Blinds shut; silence echoed in every crevice.
The world carried on, oblivious to my strife,
Cheap meals consumed, barely sustaining life.

~

They say you reap what you sow,
but the seeds I had sown, led to a tragedy I couldn't atone.
If only I could turn back the hands of time,
To relive the moments, rewrite the rhyme.

~

Yet, in this dark abyss, forgiveness emerged,
A flicker of hope, where sadness had surged.
For in forgiving myself, I found strength anew,
A journey of healing, a path to pursue.

~

Each day a step forward, no longer held back,
In the face of adversity, no longer off track.
Learning to smile again, a slow but sure climb,
Leaving behind the guilt, embracing life's chime.

~

Still living but questions remain,
What awaits beyond, what will life contain?
The hardest part may be over, but the journey's not done,
Leaving me wondering, what's next to be spun.

In the Shadows of Mortality

Time: 03:57
Date: 28/11/23

Strangely enough, throughout my life,
Death was always close,
But it didn't really happen to people I loved the most.

~

From when I was a child, seeing a man set on fire burning,
As little as I was, I knew that this was concerning.
Then growing up, death started returning,
A car crash in front of my house,
Killing someone else as they were working.

~

Then there Roshawn lied, dead in a car crash,
This was after telling me he was coming to see me in a flash.

~

Then there was my brother who died in a hospital,
Seconds before my mother called me,
How was that logical?

~

Death continues around me, all the time,
Leaving me to wonder, is it a sign?

~

Am I cursed or just unlucky, I pondered each day,
Why does Death follow me, every step of the way?

~

I tried to distance myself, to break the spell,
But Death had its grip, and I couldn't tell.

~

Was it fate or mere coincidence, this morbid connection?
I couldn't find answers, no matter my introspection.
As years went by, I learned to live with the shadow,
Embracing the uncertainty, letting fate row.

~

But still, I wondered,
Why was death my constant companion?
Was there a reason, a purpose, hidden in this union?

~

And then there was my best friend Shermaine,

Another death close to me, but for this one, I felt the pain.
This death was a death that I could not contain,
I didn't even know how I would remain.

~

Death continues around me, but mostly now in my sleep,
I see people I know, dead on the concrete.
My father, my grandmother, it's like this story was already written,
But why me? Why am I put in this position?

~

What connection do I have with death?
I am still trying to find out; I just don't know yet.

~

Days turned into nights, and nights into days,
My mind plagued with visions that continually replayed.
I became an insomniac,
Fearing the moment I'd close my eyes,
For in my dreams, there was no escape from the demise.

~

Every night, I wandered through an ethereal land,
Where ghosts of the deceased stretched out their hands.
They whispered secrets, long-buried truths,
But understanding them seemed beyond my youth.

In the Arms of the Breeze

Time: 23:37
Date: 28/11/23

Have you ever felt the wind's gentle touch?
The way it caresses your face, oh, so much.
It's a feeling that makes my heart skip a beat,
As I stand still, in awe, on the bustling street.

~

There's something magical about the breeze,
It whispers secrets through the rustling trees.
It dances and twirls, with a playful grace,
Leaving a smile on my lips, a trace.

~

It sweeps me off my feet, to my surprise,
A gentle force that makes me close my eyes.
I'm captivated by its enchanting spell,
An embrace I never want to bid farewell.

~

On scorching days, when the heat is intense,
The wind is my savior, my only defense.
It brushes against my skin, a cool embrace,
Relieving the sweat, bringing solace and grace.

~

But it's by the seaside where I find pure bliss,
As the wind whips through my hair with a gentle hiss.
The salty air, the crashing waves, the sandy shore,
A symphony of nature that I simply adore.

~

But the wind, oh, it's a mystery untold,
It carries whispers of stories, both new and old.
As I stand here, feeling its invisible touch,
I can't help but wonder, what hides within its clutch?

~

Does it carry the dreams of those who dare,
To chase their aspirations, without a care?

Or does it carry the sorrows, the tears,
Of those burdened by worries, their greatest fears.
~

The wind keeps its secrets, guarded with care,
Leaving me curious, with unanswered prayer.
But that's the beauty of this invisible force,
It leaves me longing, craving, wanting more, of course.
~

So, the next time the wind gently kisses your face,
Embrace its presence, let yourself be embraced.
For within its whispers and delicate breeze,
Lies a world of wonder, waiting to appease.
~

And as I stand here, feeling the wind's gentle tease,
It makes me stop for a second and freeze.
There's something about it that puts me at ease,
The sight as I am looking at the trees.
~

But the wind, it's a story, forever untold,
Leaving me captivated, craving its hold.
So, as I bid farewell, with a lingering sigh,
I'll forever wonder what secrets; the wind has to hide.

Love's Serendipity

Time: 23:59
Date: 28/11/23

I found myself dreaming of love, up and down.
It was time for me to go on a date,
To find my future husband, my soulmate.

~

Excitement filled my heart, as I imagined his embrace,
And the joy that would light up his handsome face.
I couldn't help but smile at the thought,
Of sharing meals together, the battles we fought.

~

Though our tastes may differ, we'd compromise,
For in love, it's the little things that harmonize.
I yearned to find my husband, my forever,
Through all types of weather, always together.

~

But until that day arrives, I'll keep pushing through,
On my journey to success, with dreams anew.
With determination in my eyes, and my head down,
I'll navigate life's challenges, avoiding any frown.

~

Through days of triumph and moments of strife,
I'll keep my sights set on a rewarding life.
For each step I take brings me closer to the one,
Who will make my heart sing, who'll be my rising sun.

~

So, as I wait for fate to intertwine our paths,
I'll cherish this time, avoiding any aftermaths.
For the anticipation of love is a beautiful thing,
A feeling that makes my soul dance and sing.

~

Will the journey lead to the love I desire?
Or will it be a tale that sparks further fire?

~

With curiosity piqued, I'll long for more,
To witness the happily ever after I'll adore.

But alas, dear reader, the ending I'll keep,
For love is a mystery that's hard to sweep.
~
So let your imagination run wild and free,
As you ponder the possibilities that could be.
May this tale inspire you to seek love's light,
And embrace the journey with all your might.

The Final Reckoning

Time: 00:32
Date: 26/11/23

In the silent hours of midnight,
Nestled on my sofa's warm invite,
I found myself contemplating the unending finite.
A curious thought, a peculiar plight,
How, oh how, will I put death right?

~

Each heartbeat like a ticking clock,
A fading echo in the endless night.
Will I see you again, in that realm of ethereal light?
Will our fingers entwine, will I hold you as tight?

~

Are you taller now, have you taken flight?
Or are you a whisper in the wind, a star shining bright?
These questions flicker, a haunting kite,
In the realm of my mind where grief ignites.

~

Sometimes, I wonder how death tastes,
Sweet or bitter, a frosty white?
Does it cradle gently, or clench in spite?
Do you wail in agony, or sigh in delight?
When tugging at life's thread, does it even feel right?

~

Do your eyes close to birth a celestial sight?
Does the universe explode into a sphere of light?
Or is it a quiet goodbye, vanishing into the night?
God, please tell me, satisfy my appetite.

~

Often, I ponder how the afterlife unfurls,
Is it a heaven painted in swirls?
Or does hell blaze, where despair twirls?
Will God welcome me, or let the abyss unfurl?

~

Will I dance on clouds, will rivers of joy twirl?
Or will I be a fallen angel, if that's the divine herald?
Will I bask in heavenly glow, a precious pearl?
Or will the fiery pits, my fate unfurl?

~
The abyss of the unknown, vast and wide,
Keeps me gazing at the star-studded tide.
Yet as dawn breaks, I take it all in stride,
For even in questions, hope resides.
~
As the morning sun begins to glide,
These midnight musings set aside,
I realize, only in living, can these answers abide.
So, I embrace the day, and let the unknown slide.
~
For in the end, we all will ride,
In death's carriage towards the other side.
Will we continue, or will existence divide?
The answer it seems, will forever hide.

Mindful Retreat

Time: 01:35
Date: 27/11/23

In the labyrinth of my own curiosity,
During a quest to comprehend your complex mentality,
Somehow, I found myself navigating the unpredictable waters
Of a mental health facility.

~

For the first time, I faced the raw humanity,
Stripped of life's usual stability,
Those clad in sorrow and confusion,
Their minds held hostage, bodies dwindling in mobility.

~

The incessant wailing echoed, lonely voices screaming, their
Existence shrinking to an echoing shouting,
Many bewildered and lost, not aware of their surroundings,
Their reality constantly doubting.

~

It was a realm where normalcy morphed into a phantom,
A concept more daunting than death,
An eerie world, a chaotic chorus of minds,
Where sanity was a fleeting breath.

~

They needed more than a roof over their head,
A mere physical housing,
They needed a touch of empathy,
A support system during their emotional winter's dowsing.

~

Yet, the world continued spinning,
Largely ignorant, their struggles unobserved,
Such cruel fate was undeserved,
A silent war against a disease unnerved.

~

Deaf to pleas, blind to tears,
Mental health snatches away the sparkle in one's eyes,
It doesn't discriminate, doesn't care about your nationality,
Not even if you're Chinese or spies.

~
The stark realization of this grim plight,
echoed through the long and lonely nights,
A bitter truth, secrecy clothed in plain sight,
a societal blind-spot in the human rights.
~
And so, the tale ends not with a resolution,
But rather with an unanswered ponder,
A haunting reminder of lives lived in shadows,
A world we seldom wander.
~
Leaving us to wonder, in a world so connected yet so apart,
How many invisible battles are fought in the quiet recesses of
The human heart?

Sunday's Deadly Curse
Time: 03:19
Date: 26/11/23

Once upon a Sunday, surrounded by a gentle mist,
I lost another soul; it's a moment I can't resist.
Not on a Monday, nor other days of the week,
It's Sundays when life's tapestry begins to tweak.

~

After your departure, my eyes were forced wide open,
A view upon reality, a truth hard to be spoken.
If death were to knock again on my somber door,
Surprise wouldn't grip my heart anymore.

~

Curiously, when someone journeys to the beyond,
A sensation rumbles in my core, an eerie silent bond.
It's a stirring that ascends, a spiritual diagnosis,
My soul's ascension, syncing with the process.

~

Death, it seems, plays a wicked game of hide and seek,
It creeps silently among us, preying on the weak.
It takes them without warning,
Without a chance to say goodbye.
Leaving behind a trail of memories that make us sigh.

~

Shermaine, my brother, strong and brave,
Once filled our lives with laughter,
Not a soul they couldn't save.
Roshawn, the sun of my heart, his light was truly bright,
In every corner of our world, he brought sheer delight.

~

The depth of this anguish is hard to confine,
Every Sunday morning, their absence underlines.
Yet, in every tender remembrance, their spirits come alive.
In those fleeting moments, they're no longer deprived.

~
I've come to understand death's place in this life of ours,
It's a twist in the tale,
A fallen star from the heavens' bower.
I've missed them, yes,
But their memories are a sweet tune.
For now, I bear the Sundays, knowing I'll join them soon.
~
Engulfed by this revelation, I watch the Sunday sunrise.
A knowing smile adorns my face; I wear it as my disguise.
I await the day, whenever it may arise,
When I meet them at the end of our earthly ties.
~
For now, life meanders like rivers to the sea,
Each Sunday a stepping stone, an echo of thee.
As the sunsets, I let myself wonder,
When the next Sunday arrives, who will it take, I ponder.

The Weight Debate

Time: 21:55
Date: 28/11/23

In a world, where judgments fly high,
There's a whispering voice, with a heavy sigh.
They would often call me skinny, to poke some fun,
Assuming it wouldn't hurt anyone.

~

Akin to the sentiments of Big Fat Jimmy,
Who's ridiculed for not being trim and slimmy.
"Hey, don't you shy away from a tasty morsel!"
They'd chide, as if it were some sweet parental counsel.

~

I'd dream of a day when one such soul,
Devoid of biases, with empathy as their goal.
Would share with me, their candid tale,
Of living life on a larger scale.

~

Big enough to make heels cower,
Their belly fat commanding power.
How the pleasures of succulent meals,
Pacify their emotional ordeals.

~

Then, maybe I'd understand their joy, their sorrow,
And not dread the coming of tomorrow.
For the "big" ones and the "skinny", it's all the same,
We're just pawns in life's peculiar game.

~

Their words, caustic, each an arrow,
Piercing through the marrow.
In silence, I'd endure the taunts,
Feeling their veiled emotional haunts.

~

No, I don't need your pity-laden glances,

Your unneeded dietary stances.
Perhaps, you'd fare better with a doctor's note,
Or a therapist's empathetic quote.
~
In this tapestry of diverse threads,
There lies a commonality that dreads.
The judgmental looks, the unsolicited advice,
Why can't acceptance be our only device?

Embracing Arborophilia

Time: 08:04
Date: 22/11/23

Can I tell you how much I'm in love with trees?
Let me share a story that will surely appease.
It all began on a bright autumn day,
When I decided to venture out and play.

~

I strolled through a forest, surrounded by foliage so grand,
And as I walked, I could feel the magic firsthand.
The leaves danced around me, rustling with delight,
As they showcased their vibrant shades under the sunlight.

~

My eyes were drawn to a majestic oak,
standing tall and proud like a regal folk.
Its branches stretched out, reaching for the sky,
And in that moment, I couldn't help but sigh.

~

I continued my journey, exploring the woods,
admiring the trees in all their various moods.
From the mighty redwoods, towering with grace,
To the delicate cherry blossom tree's embrace.

~

Each tree had a story, a tale to be told,
Of the wonders and secrets they each unfold.
Some had been witnesses to history's past,
While others provided shelter to creatures so vast.

~

I couldn't help but notice a weeping willow,
Its branches swaying gently, as if to bestow.
A sense of calmness washed over me,
As if the tree whispered, "Come, rest beneath me."

~

As the day drew closer to its end,
I found myself pondering, my thoughts on trees extend.
They're more than just wood, leaves, and bark,
They're guardians of nature, leaving their mark.

~
For when the world seems chaotic and tough,
The trees stand tall, steadfast and enough.
They remind us of life's simple grace,
And the importance of finding our own space.
~
So, if you ever feel lost or out of whack,
Turn to the trees, follow their track.
They'll guide you back to where you belong,
Their branches embracing you, forever strong.
~
And with every season that comes and goes,
The trees continue to thrive and compose.
An endless symphony of colours and hues,
Captivating our hearts, enlightening our views.
~
In this ode to trees, I'll leave it unsaid,
The mysteries they hold, the beauty they spread.
So, go for a walk, gaze upon their majesty,
And discover the love for trees that sets your spirit free.

Life

Time: 08:51
Date: 22/11/23

Tell me what's fair,
To live in a life of struggle or to be breathing air?
These words echoed in my head as I walked down the street,
Thinking about all the obstacles life had thrown at my feet.

~

I remembered the days when I was just a child,
Everything was so simple and life was mild.
But as I grew older, the world became a twisted mess,
Full of violence, hatred, and distress.

~

Life can truly be a nightmare,
Especially when you're met with people who don't care.
They'll judge and they'll lie, while they watch you and stare,
And then record it and put it on social media to share.

~

I've seen people suffer from anxiety and depression,
Struggling to survive in a world of aggression.
Breathing air is not a privilege in this society,
When every day is filled with such anxiety.

~

But even in the midst of all this pain and strife,
There's a glimmer of hope that keeps me alive.
I've learned to focus on the good and ignore the bad,
And to never let the world make me feel too sad.

~

So, I'll keep on breathing and fighting every day,
And I'll never let the darkness take my hopes away.
One two three four, I'll keep going, no matter what's fair,
And I'll make sure that my life is filled with love, not despair.

The Unseen Impact

Time: 01:03
Date: 17/11/23

I, a daughter, stood in anguish and pain.
"Is this a charade?" you'd question,
With a heart that refused to pay heed,
While I stood, confronting a wound that silently bled.

~

A beacon of love, your essence, a soothing balm,
Warming hearts and conjuring smiles, oh, your charm!
Even ancestors, bound in their ethereal state,
Blushed at your benevolence, a blessing innate.

~

Isn't it captivating, this symphony of praise?
Yet, let's pull away the curtain for a closer gaze.
Amidst this chorus of accolades, there stood you, unflinching,
firm in your belief that I was always running.

~

"Look at my daughter," you'd proclaim with a smile,
"A beacon of hope, every struggle she defiles."
Yet, beneath this facade of pride and admiration,
Lay a cave of judgment, devoid of heart's conversation.

~

As a father, as my idol, you were a fortress so strong,
A haven of wisdom where dreams were woven and spun.
Yet, hidden in your stronghold was a chamber,
Cold and confined, where feelings feared to tread,
And emotions were denied.

~

Ah, the paradox of my existence, a dual dichotomy, tethered
between the love of a father and an unquenchable longing.
In the shadow of your glory, I strived,
Yearning to unveil the echo of my voice, buried and once again
denied.

~

Underneath the veneer of your stern, stoic demeanor,
Was a part of you unknown,
A realm untouched by the hand of empathy.

~

Doors were firmly closed, emotions kept at bay,
Hiding within was a soul, shrouded in shades of grey.

~

In the end, the threads of our bond, both bitter and sweet,
Wove a tapestry of life, imperfect yet replete.
In the silence of your soul, my echoes found their song,
And in the shadow of your glory, I found where I belong.

~

Yet, as the curtain falls, I can't help but wonder,
Will the doors of your heart ever burst asunder?
Will the echoes of my pain make their way to you?
My Father, my idol, if only you knew...

The Unexpected Goodbye

Time: 03:00
Date: 26/11/23

I never thought that you would leave.
Your vibrant spirit, your contagious laughter, so naive,
Even while your body laid in that hospital, I didn't believe.

~

You were the sunflower in a field, rest in an evening's reprieve,
Now children you will never conceive.
Echoes of your voice, trapped within my soul's archive,
Your hugs, our conversations, I will never receive.

~

In painful irony, the vibrant Shermaine, life chose to bereave,
Life can be so horrible; it can really deceive.
Without a warning, without a note, without a reprieve,
You left me without saying goodbye, and I will forever grieve.

~

A dream once was, now a wound that won't relieve,
Your dreams of opening a hair salon will never be achieved.
A silent whisper in the wind, a throbbing pain I perceive,
I love you, Shermaine Campbell, and I'm still in disbelief.

~

And so, the whispers of the wind carried the silent plea,
A vow of love never forgotten, from sea to endless sea.
Yet, the echoes of the unanswered cries will always be,
Leaving me to wonder, will Shermaine ever answer that plea?

Rise and Thrive

Time: 11:49
Date: 16/11/23

In the dusky silence of the early morn,
I'd pray down on my knees, beseeching for the dawn.
Clouds of uncertainty cloaked my soul,
A voiceless plea trapped in a sprawling black hole.

~

The Lord, my Lord, seemed distant as a star,
Ensnared in my strife, my life stood bizarre.
The world outside hustled, buzzing and bright,
Yet the echo of My silence marked my endless nights.

~

Through the darkest abyss,
Tasha Cobbs and Cici Winans enkindled my spirit,
Their harmonious whispers, my pain could inherit.
Yet, even the songs of succor seemed alien and sealed,
As life's cruel jest, in my heart continually revealed.

~

Broken, exhausted, I felt my will sway,
Life was a game I no longer wished to play.
The gleam of the sharp knife, a morbid allure,
Yet, a vision of my future held me from the precipice, pure.

~

The certainty of a love unknown, the promise of being a wife,
Withheld me from plunging into the afterlife.
To burn forever in the fiery pits of hell,
Was a destiny I was determined to quell.

~

Every morning was a battle, each step a war,
Dragging myself from the comfort of the bedroom floor.
Amid the struggles, the sorrow, the unshed tears,
Against the urge to surrender to my primal fears.

~

Disillusionment wasn't my fate,
Nor the despairing choice to be a whore's duplicate.
Despite the odds, I held my head high,
Refusing to let my dreams die.

~

As the sun dipped down, the moon began to glow,
Waves of night draped the world below.
In the silence of my thoughts, in the quiet of the night,
I found myself within, a source of radiant light.

~

In the heartache, the pain and the despair,
I found the strength to breathe, to hope and to dare.
For within me, I discovered a resilience unbowed,
A woman fierce, unbroken, and proud.

~

A tale of my life, etched in scars and in strife,
A testament to my willingness to thrive.
With the break of dawn, a new day beckoned,
A new chance to confront whatever life reckoned.

~

The journey was long, but I stood,
Unbowed and strong,
A song of triumph was my life's unfolding song.

The Mighty Pen

Time: 06:33
Date: 28/11/23

Beneath the dimmed glow of an old study lamp,
I sat, my pen poised over the parchment as the clock struck midnight.

~

The room was filled with silence, the only sound was the
Rhythmic tapping of my impatient pen against the wooden desk.

~

A long-forgotten story, trapped within my soul was yearning to breathe through the ink of my pen. And then it came, not as the Thunderous flood I expected, but as a steady, rhythmic trickle.

~

"One month of relentless writing,"
I whispered to the silent room, looking around at the chaos of Crumpled paper and ink smudges. Every word, every comma, Every letter was shaped from the raw power of emotions that Coursed through my veins. Each line was a puzzle, fitting Perfectly into the next, forming a beautiful symphony of words.

~

A poem bloomed, and I was its gardener. As one verse faded, Another took its place, like waves crashing against the shore, One endlessly chasing the other. Unveiling years of pain, years Of silent tears, every word felt like a sigh of relief, a burden lifted.

~

I hadn't planned on creating this masterpiece forged from the Fire of my soul. My pen, once idle, found its purpose as if by Divine intervention and twirled across the pages, Leaving behind a trail of my story.

~

The shock of it was numbing. I had forgotten the intoxicating Power of writing, the rush of words, the emotions, and the sheer Joy of bringing a story to life. But as the words flowed, I realized That my pen, was indeed my rock.

~
Three long years of silence, of a voice stifled and words lost.
Returning was like coming home after a long journey, familiar,
Yet surprisingly new. This time, however, the stakes were
Higher. It wasn't just about pouring my heart into words
anymore, it was also about making a living.
~
Creating a book felt like weaving a spell, each word a thread
Drawn from the depth of my soul, intricately woven into a
Tapestry of tales. But as I closed the book, my heart pounded
With anticipation and fear. Would the world accept my tapestry
Of tales? Would they see beyond the rhymes and rhythms to
The story hidden beneath?
~
With a newfound resolve, I looked at my finished work. The
pages, filled with my heart's musings, stared back, promising a
Journey into a soul-wrenching narrative. The ink was dry, the
Words set in their eternal dance.
~
The journey of my book had ended, yet, another was about to
Begin - in the hands of the world, under their scrutinizing gaze,
Ripe for their discerning tastes. What will they find, reading
Between my lines? Will they see the phoenix rising through my
Words, or will they merely perceive a hollow echo?
~
A curious bewilderment lingered in the silence of the room as I
Pondered these thoughts. The world was on the brink of a
Journey through my words,
And what lay beyond that final period, only time would reveal.

Preserving the Sacred

Time: 05:14
Date: 19/11/23

In a world of chaos and deceit,
Where love is a game and trust is obsolete,
Men and women play their part,
Using their bodies to satisfy their heart.
But amidst the madness and the sin,
I choose to stay true to the light within.

~

I step away from the worldly haze,
Seeking clarity in these bewildering days.
For I refuse to be swayed by lust's call,
I cherish my soul, I'll never fall.

~

The flesh is fleeting, its desires will wane,
The spirit within has so much to gain.
I turn to the Bible, seeking wisdom and truth,
I find solace in its age-old sleuth.

~

As I walk this path with faith as my guide,
I leave the temptations of the world aside.
But as I ponder the choices I've made,
I wonder if my resolve will begin to fade.

~

Will I be lured by the worldly charm,
Or will I stay steadfast, free from harm?
The answers elude me, keeping me in suspense,
As I navigate this world, devoid of pretense.

~

In a world full of chaos, where love is a game,
I strive to remain pure, untainted by shame.
The journey ahead remains unseen,
But I'll hold onto hope, my spirit serene.

~

So, I tread with caution, my spirit unflawed,
As I navigate this world, still in awe.

To Death, We All Owe

Time: 00:19
Date: 26/11/23

In the mist of time and the velvet void,
I began a journey of healing, life unfurled and uncoiled.
Amidst the ticking clock, I pondered deep,
how swiftly life slips away, in silence, without a peep.

~

Car crashes, cancers, and brain damage too,
Death wears many faces, grim and rue.
An array of paths to the end so long,
Each bringing forth that final, mournful song.

~

In the hush of night when most are strong,
Some meet their end, their lives drawn along.
Families huddled in sorrow, their hearts draped in grey,
While their favourite melodies at the funeral play.

~

Strokes, diabetes, and arteries tired and worn,
Life's battle-battered warriors, their vitality shorn.
Or perhaps a bullet's fury or a tragic careless fall,
Oh, the many ways death can call.

~

Just a blink, a breath, a fleeting ebb,
And one is swept away, life's intricate web.
Like a fallen leaf carried by the breeze,
A life is whisked away with a startling ease.

~

And the grim truth that none can flee,
Life's only certainty, its unyielding decree.
With every sunrise and moon's soft glow,
One truth stands firm - to death, we all owe.

~

In this dance between birth and death,
Let our moments be savored, each breath.
For the end comes swiftly, silently it creeps,
And in the blink of an eye, it's forever sleep.

~
Thus, on this healing journey, wisdom unfolds,
Cherish each moment before the final bell tolls.
For life's cruel joke, its last laugh it seems,
Is that no matter what, we all pay life's death fees.

Lost in the Noise

Time: 03: 54
Date: 20/11/23

It's not that I was running, I just had to be free,
I needed time out to get to know the real ME!

~

The days had blurred together, like colours in the rain,
And I realized I needed solitude, a moment to escape the pain.
I need time to heal, I needed time to see,
What my future would look like, what would I be?

~

As the world searched for me, with worry in their eyes,
I wandered through the wilderness, under the open skies.
I heard you guys were looking for me, you even got the police
And the rest of the family tree. It really wasn't in my intentions
To flee, and it didn't take one year, or two years, it took three.

~

I found solace in the silence, in the whispers of the breeze,
And In the dance of the stars, I Finally found my ease.
I discovered strength within, I found courage deep inside,
And as time stood still, I let go of my pride.

~

Now, as I stand before you, with the past fading into the night,
I realize that the journey was the destination,
The struggle was the fight.

~

So, as I vanish into the horizon, with a smile upon my face,
I leave you with this question - was I really lost,
Or was I found in this embrace?

~

And as the echoes of my footsteps fade into the blue,
I leave you with a mystery, a tale that feels all too true.
For in the end, perhaps I wasn't lost at all,
But just a soul in search of peace, standing tall.

The Journey to Wholeness

Time: 04:21
Date: 19/11/23

I lost all my weight, my body was shutting down,
If I carried on like this, I would be in the ground.
It's not like I wanted this, I wasn't trying to look like a clown,
But the thought of you dying, made me feel like I would drown.

~

So, I sought help, I went and got therapy,
The first time I saw that therapist,
I thought, this will end terribly.
It took me months to open up,
Because her so-called healing was temporarily,
But somehow, she got me, and it was extraordinary.

~

There were tears, there were happiness,
But she asked me why wasn't I angry?
But why would I be, if I knew the truth quite frankly.

~

As I sat in her office, I felt a shift inside,
The weight of the world, I no longer needed to hide.
She helped me see, the strength that I hold,
And in that moment, a new story began to unfold.

~

Now I stand here, lighter in body and soul,
Thanks to the therapist, who helped make me whole.
But the curious thing, that still leaves me wondering,
What if she was the one, who needed the mending?

~

It was evident to see that therapy works,
Because here I am finally able to make a little smirk.

Invisible Battles

Time: 02:07
Date: 17/11/23

In the quiet depths of anguish, where truth is hard to glean,
Lived I, a soul embroiled in torment unseen.
A cynic, skeptic, heart aflame in mounting doubt,
It wasn't that I closed my heart, just that faith had stepped out.

~

Anger, like a voracious beast, coursed through my veins,
Mocking mankind's mortal coil, its transient gains.
In every face, a hollow mask, a cold, skin-deep facade,
Longing for the world to change, in silence, I nodded.

~

Against the tumult of my mind, a prayer found its way,
More like a desperate bargain with the Lord, if I dare say.
To leave this world not in sin's grip, my spirit yearned,
Despite the bridges behind me that I'd willingly burned.

~

In solitude, I wrapped myself, a refuge from the world,
Depression, loneliness, my silent cries,
Through the darkness I swirled.
I danced with despair like a lover lost, twirled in its embrace,
Choking on the bitter truth, life was but a rat race.

~

Then in the face of the inevitable, acceptance dawned on me,
Life, death, struggle—it's survival of the fittest you see.
The light of acknowledgment ignited my spirit's core,
For even in the heart of chaos, life holds something more.

~

And so, my tale ends here, yet begins anew,
With lessons etched in shadows, and truths in sorrow's hue.
In life's grand theatre, no act is ever wasted,
Only the strongest souls survive, the weak, by struggles, are tested.

~

So here I stand at the edge of the unknown,
The void before me vast,
Realizing that the hardest times have already passed.
But this tale isn't over, it's merely at a bend,
Leaving you to ponder, where will my journey end?

~

Even today, you are always on my mind,

Don't worry Shermaine, I'm staying on my grind.

The Healing Power of the Gym

Time: 01:37
Date: 17/11/23

I remember when I was fully in my prime,
I found myself at a crossroads,
Parallel to the rhythm of a rhyme.
The beams of gleaming neon lights,
Painted a picture in the hazy night.
A gym was my refuge, my purgatory, my place to fight.

~

A treadmill stood before me,
As daunting as a mountain's height,
Reflecting back the image of a spirit still sparkling bright.
Tears filled my eyes, saltier than a sea,
As I stepped onto the treadmill, yearning for a moment of glee.

~

Each squat, each lunge, each grueling stride,
Was a battle waged against the melancholy trapped inside.
Tears streaming down my cheeks, a silent, sorrowful outcry,
Each day gaining strength, I had no choice but to comply.

~

You were no longer with me, but your image haunted my mind,
Your laughter echoed in my ears, a melody rewind.
I wished I had said goodbye, but I was far too shy,
Now, gazing at the sky, I could only let out a sigh.

~

Beside the tranquil river under the moon's silver glow,
I felt your presence accompanying my sorrow.
In the silent whispers of the wind, I heard your voice,
I can hear it so clearly, even above the rumbling noise.

~

Was it my doing? Was it a result of my deeds?
Did I unwittingly plant these heart-wrenching seeds?
Days blurred into nights in an endless, tormented sigh,
Craving to escape reality, sometimes I wanted to get high.

~

The rehab was hard, a test of endurance.
But with each passing day, I was breaking my own silence.
My strength I had to supply, each day, each night,
It wasn't about the gym anymore; it was about a personal fight.

~

I rose from the ashes, stronger than ever before.
The pain was a memory, the victory was much more.
But now, I don't return to the gym,
My battles are no longer fought there.
For life is a great teacher, it made me aware.
~
Now, I'm a warrior without the weights,
Stronger in mind and soul.
My body, a testament of resilience, for I've embraced a new role.
Fitness is more than just lifting,
Running, and jumping high,
It's a state of mind, a spirit that can't be embodied by a mere thigh.
~
I've learned the hard way, a lesson that's hard to buy.
The journey's all worth it, the strength you have to supply,
But to the gym, I ain't going back, I don't need to modify,
For I'm not just a body, I am someone that wants to live in the sky.
~
A story of a girl who fell only to rise,
Who faced her fears to claim her prize,
The gym was just a stage, but life, is the real exercise.

Despairful Silence

Time: 05:01
Date: 28/11/23

As a child, I recall the echoing sound of your laughter,
Reverberating in my ears like the distant rolling of thunder.
Your heart, untouched by malice or deceit,
Pure as the finest gold. A lion's courage was in your spirit.
Your kindness radiated like the sun's bold rays.
But now, I shiver in the bitter cold, alone,
Waiting for something that's never going to come.

~

Three years have circled round the sun,
And yet my life, it feels so stalled.
My soul's caught in this chilling cold,
Forever hinging onto the echoes of your bold laughter,
Your golden heart.
We used to jest about how old we were becoming,
Believing time was on our side, but mortality had other plans.

~

You never even touched three decades.
Life was swift and cruel; it didn't give you time to flourish,
To form into the woman, you were destined to become.
Would I trade all my tomorrows for just one more day with you? Without hesitation, I would. If death could be delayed, if
Life could be tethered, if only...

~

But alas, this is not a tale of life, resplendent in glitter and gold.
It's a story woven from the threads of death, of aching voids and
Crushing pain. It's an ode to strength born from grief, an
Anthem of resilience ringing out from the depths of despairful silence.

~

We used to dream of seizing the stars, but now I reach out only
To clutch the empty air. Your absence is a void, a vast,
Consuming black hole that swallows my dreams and hopes,
Leaving me in darkness. Yet, I find solace in the memories we
Etched together, the shared laughter and playful banter, the
Heartfelt talks under the starlit sky.

You live within these fragments of time,
Stitched into the fabric of my existence.

~

So here I am, amidst this world, waiting in the cold,
Your laughter still resonating in my ears, your golden heart
Forever etched in my soul.
Time may have ceased for you, but your memory is immortal,
pulsating through the veins of my existence.

~

And now, as I stand at the edge of tomorrow, I wonder... where
Are you in the cosmos? Are you the sun that warms my face?
Are you the evening breeze that whispers through the trees?
Or perhaps, you are the unseen force that guides my path,
The invisible hand that holds me when I stumble,
The silent voice that speaks to my soul.

~

As the storybook of my life continues to unfold, every
Succeeding chapter whispers your name, echoing your laughter,
Resonating your kindness. And the final page? Oh, that remains
Unwritten, leaving me, and you, dear reader, wondering - what
Lies beyond the silence of the final full stop?

Whew Who knew

Time: 13:44
Date: 28/10/23

Whew, who knew!
That I was going to fall in love with YOU!
~
I loved you because you were YOU!
The electricity in your touch beats on cue.
~
With each sunrise, my love for you grows,
Like an unending river, perennially it flows.
~
And yes, I love it, strange it may seem,
When you pick your nose, in solitude or gleam.
~
With you, there's no facade or pretense,
Our love, it defies common sense.
~
I relish when you feed me food,
Each bite, a testament to our love's magnitude.
~
The sweetness, the spice, the flavours burst,
Our love story, a romantic first.
~
But know this, I'm spoilt and a bit toxic,
In your love, I found a perfect mix.
~
You've seen my flaws, yet you remain so strong,
In your arms, I feel I belong.

Lessons in Love

Time: 10: 53
Date: 09/11/23

In the bitter silence, we stood face to face,
Our love unravelling, leaving not a trace.
Words like knives, cutting deep with each retort,
Tearing my world asunder, breaking my fragile fort.

~

At dinner, the taste of pain lingered in the air,
As we feigned normalcy, pretending not to care.
Along the riverbank, where love once bloomed strong,
Now echoed with heartache, a haunting, sorrowful song.

~

Broken and bruised, I had to find my way,
Through the darkness, I pushed through, day by day.
Five months of solitude, of growth and inner strife,
I emerged stronger, ready to embrace a new life.

~

But now you're back, knocking on my door,
And I'm torn, uncertain, afraid to endure.
The scars you left run deep, etched within my core,
I fear the pain of losing, of being hurt once more.

~

Yet, a part of me remains guarded and wise,
Never again to succumb to lovesick cries.
I'll hold onto my strength, never again to deceive,
For once broken, now mended,
I'll never wear my heart on my sleeve.

~

You broke me and in silence I accepted my peace,
my old self who was once carefree now filled with grief.

~

But that's okay, because love has taught me so much,
To always stay pure and stay untouched.

Love's Souvenirs

Time: 14:34
Date: 28/10/23

In the moody lamplight,
I shimmered like a glistening jewel,
A sight too enticing, making you drool.
You sat back, a detached observer,
Awaiting on the show's release,
Your eyes gleamed with happiness,
Almost as if you were watching a masterpiece.

~

Every crevice of the room echoed with anticipated silence,
I was in the body of someone else,
"Someone stole my license."

~

Legs wide open, you couldn't wait to relish in my richness,
Your eyes, they were impatient,
Wanting to commit and bear witness.

~

Your gaze was filled with desire,
Oh, how it set my heart ablaze,
In the face of your longing, my resistance began to fade.

~

As you sat up on the bed, powerful and grand,
You looked like God Zeus, holding fate in your hand.

~

In a world where the night held its embrace,
I rose from my solitude; my heart began to race.
Shaking off the shroud of uncertainty that encased,
I stood up, meandering across the room, your face was my chase.

~

With fervour in my stride and determination in my pace,
I walked over to you, a scene our fate had traced.

~

There you were, under the luminous glow of the chandelier lace,
An aura of calm that had my nerves misplaced.

As if possessed by a force, magnetic, and ace,
I found myself drawn to you, caught in a sudden embrace.
~
There, I sat on your face,
You welcomed me with open arms, no hint of disgrace.
Whispering against the silence, "Fuck breathing space,
And just in case I die, ride it with grace."
~
Conventional norms screamed,
Calling our actions a disgrace,
Yet there was a sacred sanctity in this uncharted space.
All doubts erased, passion took their place,
From the touch of your hands,
To the warmth of our interlaced.
To the world, we were sinners drawn to the forbidden
base, our love an erratic rhythm, a reckless pace.
~
But in the shroud of the night,
You were my solace, my saving grace.
From the caress of your hands to the tenderness of your
Lips, you were my happy place.
~
Now, it was my turn, on my knees, I would pray,
For the strength to take the stage in my own way.
Pleasuring you was my fortitude,
It was like I was working on Broadway,
The cheers and applause were my only pay.
~
I tongue danced with words,
Like an artist paints with his brush,
Every verb, and noun was to make you blush.
~
In the sea of letters, I found my peace,
Making sense of the chaos, my solace, your release.
Every tap of the tongue, like a melody,
My fingers were the dancers in this symphony.
~
The world was a stage, and I was writing the play,
Becoming every character, in every possible way.
The hero, the villain, the lover, the clown,
I played them all, not once did I ever back down.

Unveiling the Reality

Time: 20:02
Date: 19/11/23

In a world where the truth became deception,
They pushed us all to seek protection.
No reflections in the mirror could be found,
As they told us to line up and be bound.

~

The injection they said would set us free,
But the doubt and fear remained inside of me.
Lies spun like a web to provoke our reaction, while the Government turned a blind callous fraction.

~

No jobs, no work, just COVID detections,
Creating a haze of unanswered questions.
People who were once healthy and whole,
Now had no recollection of their own soul.

~

The news and media painted a story of perfection,
While we drowned in this deceptive infection.
Families torn apart, loved ones left alone,
Their bodies used as a mere stepping stone.

~

And when they were done, discarded without affection,
Thrown out like trash, a brutal disconnection.
The world seemed to accept it all without objection,
Leaving us haunted by this cruel, heartless infection.

~

But in the silence, a whisper of truth remained,
The mysteries and secrets yet to be unchained.
For in the darkness, a light still flickers on,
A glimmer of hope for the truth to dawn.

~

The story they told may have seemed complete,
But something deeper lies beneath the deceit.
So let us question, seek, and never rest,
For the truth is waiting, longing to manifest.

My Soul's Melody

Time: 00:01
Date: 17/11/23

Once upon a time, a tale steeped in the quill's ink stain,
I had my words, my sweet refrain,
Then silence came as an uninvited guest,
Learning to write again, I embarked on this challenging quest.

~

Kerry stood tall, brimming with tales of yore,
Carol, draped in metaphors, had stories, oh so raw.
Sandra, a painter of words, brought reality to her lore,
Ben, the businessman, danced with verses on every floor.

~

Yet, in the grand theatre of my mind,
The words fluttered, restless, and unkind,
An echo of whispers, a melody I couldn't unwind.
Seven published books, my testament, now seemed far behind,
In the playground of literature, I was lost, confined.

~

Once, words flowed like a river, now a stagnant fen,
Tears blotted my parchment, I was back to counting to ten.
Empty pages stared back, bearing the weight of my pen,
With a heart heavy and sinking, I wondered, when... just when?

~

When will my soul's melody find its rhythm again?
When will my mind's storm give way to a calming rain?
With each passing second, each tick of disdain,
The longing deepened, the silence became my bane.

~

But then, I realized the journey had been my muse,
In every struggle, every tear, there was a story to fuse.
Each silent moment, each word I did lose,
Was a stepping stone to the path I did choose.

~

As I closed my eyes, a prayer formed, gentle as a hymn,
A plea to the divine, a cry from within.
I sought strength to begin, to let words in,
"Lord," I whispered in the quiet night, "let this be my win."

~

For the struggle of creation is known only by a few.
Dear reader, will the words come, will they break through?
In the silence of the night, I leave this thought with you.

Seeking Answers After Death

Time: 02:14
Date: 26/11/23

Two days after you died,
We sat and talked in the shadows of the night,
Your voice a whispering echo, a chilling yet comforting sight.
You confessed your confusion, your eyes lost in distant thought,
Wondering why those mourning now,
In life, had cared for naught.

~

"Why do they cry rivers, as if they truly missed my being?
When I trembled on life's edge,
Their affection remained unseen."
Your words floated in the cold air, a sad tune on repeat,
Your puzzling queries hung in the hollow,
Where silence and sorrow meet.

~

Through the frost-covered glass door,
I watched your coffin lay,
An image so heart-wrenching,
It painted my world in dismal gray.

~

The sight seared through my heart, tore through my very core,
I listened to your spectral voice, but I couldn't take it anymore.

~

You seemed like your old self, a ghost from a time gone by,
Your laugh was like an old record, that made my soul sigh.
The memory of your liveliness clashed with the deathly scene,
Then I woke up to reality, where you could no longer be seen.

~

The dream of our conversation, the ghost of your familiar tone,
In the harsh daylight, it was clear, I was undeniably alone.
Your words still lingered, reminders of our past rapport,
The echoes of our last exchange, a bittersweet encore.

~

Staring at the glass door, there was silence instead of a tale,

The coffin sat undisturbed, proof that life is indeed frail.
It was a cruel reminder of how you were no longer here,
Leaving me alone in this world,
With my own shadows of fear.

~

Your curious question remained,
Unanswered, a haunting melody,
"Why did they mourn your loss,
When they neglected you in reality?"
And as I woke up from the dream,
Where your voice was a ghostly plea,
I was left with a bitter truth –
And the mystery of what could no longer be.

From Ashes to Strength

Time: 03:14
Date: 20/11/23

I've been through the fire, walked through the storm,
I've weathered the trials, my heart has been torn.
Once I had allure, a charm that could steal,
But now I'm on a journey, seeking what's real.

~

In the quiet of my space, life whispers its truth,
I long to leave behind the wreckage of my youth.
Love, passion, family, all seemed a distant dream,
As if nothing was as it truly seemed.

~

But now I stand here, still healing, not healed,
Ready to venture out into the battlefield.
For I carry the scars, a testament to my past,
Yet within me, a flicker of hope will forever last.

~

I'll step into the unknown, with courage as my shield,
Embracing the uncertainty, refusing to yield.
The future awaits with mysteries concealed,
And perhaps in that uncertainty, my fate will be unsealed.

~

So here I am, not yet whole,
For in this journey of healing, lies a story yet untold.

Transcending the Flesh's Finality

Time: 03:26
Date: 20/11/23

In the depths of my mind, a haunting truth lurks,
the Flesh knows no afterlife, it cunningly smirks.
It tempts and it teases, leading me astray,
whispering deceit in its haunting way.

~

I feel its presence in the dead of the night,
urging me to sin, to forsake what's right.
It promises pleasure, with a touch of pain,
A dance with darkness, a deal that's inhumane.

~

I hear its soft murmur, a seductive call,
Leading me down a path, destined for my fall.
It knows I have a life, a love so true and pure,
Yet it coaxes me to lie, my conscience left unsure.

~

The Flesh revels in the chaos it creates,
Entwining me in its web of tempting fates.
It knows I'll never find peace in its embrace,
For when it's done with me, it will leave no trace.

~

But as I navigate this treacherous plight,
I cling to the hope that flickers so bright.
For deep within me, a spark refuses to die,
Yearning for truth, reaching for the sky.

~

The Flesh may crave my eternal burn,
But I refuse to succumb, I yearn to learn.
I'll unravel its lies, cast off its binding chains,
And reclaim the life that it seeks to maim.

~

So, dear reader, heed this cautionary tale,
Of the flesh's deceit, its relentless travail.
For in the battle between darkness and light,
The ending remains shrouded, out of sight.

~
As I tread this path, uncertain and grim,
The question remains - will the Flesh win?
Or will I break free from its insidious hold,
And write my own ending, brave and bold?

Embracing the Journey to Happiness

Time: 03:36
Date: 20/11/23

In a world where we constantly seek,
For happiness in the love we speak,
I've realized that joy is not a handout,
It's a journey within, there's no doubt.
~
Not from parents, children, or kin,
But from the depths of the soul within,
Gratitude, it's the key, where to begin?
Let go of the past, let the newness in.
~
Self-respect and love, like no other could,
If you don't, why expect others should?
Set boundaries clear, let them know,
My happiness matters, it's time to grow.
~
In this quest for inner peace,
I found myself, my worries ceased.
But as I journeyed through this trial,
I wondered, could this be my final mile?
~
For the path to happiness is paved with doubt,
And as I ponder what life's truly about,
I realize the answer may not be clear,
But perhaps, just perhaps, it's already here.
~
So I'll keep seeking, this much is true,
For happiness within, in all I do.
I've found the key, and I'll hold it tight,
But the end of this journey is not in sight.

Chevan

Time: 00:38
Date: 17/11/23

I sat alone in my room, pen in hand,
As the clock struck twelve in this far-off land.
I reflected on days gone by and my heart began to sigh,
For the things I missed, the things that had now passed me by.

~

Oh my little brother, I've missed you so much,
I miss your smile, your face, your gentle touch.

~

The good old days when innocence was our clutch,
Now you have grown, driving that clutch,
Finding your way through life and gaining your touch.

~

As your elder sister, I've taken life's test,
Fought many battles, emerged as the best.
A nine-time published writer, they say.
But note, young brother, beyond laurels, there exists a fray.

~

I wish I could see you, hold you tighter,
To fill your life with a sister's brighter laughter.
Alas, the distance between us is such,
It could make even the toughest hearts much softer.

~

In the quiet of the night, your image flickers,
And my hand reaches out instinctively to that old lighter.
I see you, baby brother, on the edge of youth,
Drawn to the flame, seeking truth.

~

'Put down that lighter,' I whisper in the wind,
There are other ways to find the light within.
Don't succumb to the night's fleeting ride,
keep your focus, let your dreams guide.

~

As my words blew into the night,
I wished with all my might that they'd find you,
Give you some insight.
To make you pause, perhaps even ignite,
A spark that would light your path right.

~

Always remember, my brother dear, that I love you from afar,
As clear as the brightest star. Even in the absence, the echo of
My heart will forever play its part.

A Poetic Ode to Love and Longing

Time: 03:32
Date/19/11/23

In the quiet of the night, as I lay in bed,
thoughts of you swirl in my head.
Weeks later, I saw you smiling,
and my heart felt like it was flying.

~

You were sitting with your parents so dear,
And I was on the phone, wishing you were near.
You told me you were okay as we spoke on video,
But deep down, I felt a sense of sorrow.

~

Just hearing your voice made my heart ache,
I wanted to hold onto it, for goodness sake.
Your parents smiled and waved at the screen,
I felt broken, lost, like living in a dream.

~

Your smile, your face, things I was craving,
But alas, you're in the ground, your name engraving.
I woke up, wishing it was true,
Just one last time to be with you.

~

I miss our school days, chilling with our crew,
How I wish I could turn back time, it's true.
Just one last time, I wouldn't feel so blue,
But reality hits hard, and I miss you.

~

Now as I sit here, thinking of you, my heart still aches,
The pain making me feel blue.
I wonder if you knew how much you meant,
How your absence left me feeling so spent.

~

This world feels different without your light,
I wish I could hold you, with all my might.
The memories of you, they'll always stay,
Leaving me wondering, why you had to go away.

Mindful Musings

Time: 05:31
Date: 21/11/23

In a world filled with chaos and despair,
Where every step feels like a burden to bear,
I find myself wondering, searching for a way,
To escape the darkness and find my own ray.

~

One, two, three, four, five, six, seven,
How many steps does it take to get to heaven?
I'm willing to take that journey,
Even if it takes me to twenty-seven.

~

For what's going on in the world right now,
I'm ready to make my confessions.
It's like everyone's on antidepressants,
Numbed by pain,
Addicted or going through demonic obsessions.

~

Humans are suffering, lost in another recession,
And we do whatever the government says, without expression.
Normal people have lost their jobs, their sense of profession,
While the world carries on pretending to be deafened.

~

In this state of despair, I embark on my quest,
To find a place where hope can truly manifest.
I pack my bags, leave behind my old life,
And set out to find answers, to escape this strife.

~

Through winding roads and treacherous paths,
I walk on, determined to break these aftermaths.
The moments of silence, the whispers in the wind,
Keep me going, pushing me forward, from within.

~

With each step, I feel the weight lifting off my chest,
As if my soul is being cleansed, slowly being blessed.
I meet strangers on my journey, who share their stories,
Each one filled with pain, but also glimmers of glory.

~

They too have sought solace, a refuge from the storm,
Searching for a higher purpose, a life that can transform.

We form a bond, united in our quest for truth,
Climbing our way up, seeking eternal youth.

~

As I reach the twenty-seventh step, I pause and reflect,
The beauty that surrounds me, the serenity, I detect.
But the stairway doesn't end here, there's something more,
A mystery unwinds, a secret to explore.

~

With renewed determination, I continue my ascent,
Not knowing what awaits, what events I will lament.
But I keep going, driven by a desire so strong,
To find the answers, to right the world's wrongs.

~

And so, dear reader, my story remains untold,
As I take each step, my curiosity unfolds.
For the journey to heaven isn't just a physical climb,
It's a quest for salvation, an unravelling of time.

~

So, how many steps does it take to reach that sacred place?
I'll keep walking, keep searching, with a smile on my face.
For in this journey, I've discovered something grand,
That heaven lies not in a destination,
But in the palm of our hand.

Awakening the Spirit

Time: 05: 42
Date: 21/11/23

In the depths of despair, I found myself on my knees,
Aching for salvation, longing for peace.
And there, in that moment, as I looked up to the skies,
I saw a figure, radiant and wise.

~

It was Christ himself, his beauty beyond compare,
A sight that left me breathless, caught in a poetic snare.
I cried out to him, my voice filled with fervent zeal,
Offering my sacrifice, my heart's desperate appeal.

~

For I knew in my soul, he had paid the ultimate price,
To save us all from darkness, to grant us eternal life.
As I rose to my feet, a sense of belonging filled my core,
Understanding the consequences of my actions before.

~

Embarking on a journey, a road less travelled,
I discovered the wonders of living as Christ unravelled.
Though it may seem mundane to some, this path I tread,
To be like Jesus is a captivating adventure that never ends.

~

Every step I take, every word I speak,
Holds the power to heal, to comfort the weak.
In my actions, I see reflections of his divine grace,
And in every moment, his love I embrace.

~

So, as I walk this road, seemingly mundane,
I am reminded of the miracles that works in Jesus' name.
An endless exploration, a lifetime of worth,
Leaving you to ponder, the mysteries of rebirth.

Purposeful Living

Time: 05:15
Date: 22/11/23

My life felt like a network error,
constantly glitching and causing distress,
Each moment a struggle, a tangled mess.

~

But in those moments of chaos, I saw her face,
Reflected back at me, in that mirror's grace.
A haunting presence, a constant reminder,
Of a life lost, a love no longer by my side.

~

Years passed by, and clarity started to emerge,
Yet, the question remained, making my heart urge.
Why couldn't God spare her, I wondered each night,
Left with no answers, only a desperate fight.

~

But at some point, you have to pick yourself back up,
No more maybes, excuses, or buts.
I vowed to carry her memory with every breath I take,
To turn my dreams into reality, for her sake.

~

Life is a journey, filled with twists and turns,
And though it may never be as good as it yearns, I'll keep
pushing forward, holding onto hope,
Knowing that within this chaos, I'll learn to cope.

~

So, as I navigate through this glitchy existence,
I'll find solace in the memories, in their persistence.
For my life may have felt like a network error,
But I'll keep searching for the answers, without any terror.

The Dreamer's Manifesto

Time: 05:28
Date: 22/11/23

In a world full of dreams and schemes,
I found myself chasing my own moonbeams.
It was time to fight for my goals and dreams,
Because I knew that life was never as good as it seems.

~

Every day, I looked around and saw the desire in people's eyes,
A burning need to be treated like Kings and Queens,
To soar high up in the skies.
But reality hit hard, like a punch from a machine,
As we toiled and worked, just like cogs in a routine.

~

I had built companies from when I was in my teens,
but this time, it was a little different, or so it seemed.
The stakes were higher, the pressure extreme,
But deep down, I knew what this means.

~

I had to dig deep, work a little harder,
Even if I kicked and screamed,
For I had a vision, a dream that gleamed.
The path was rough, the journey long,
But I pushed forward, staying strong.

~

Days turned to weeks, and weeks into months,
But I refused to let my spirit be blunted.
I worked late into the night, fueled by passion and might,
Determined to turn my dreams into reality's light.

~

There were moments of doubt,
When the world seemed to conspire,
Trying to extinguish my fire.
But I held on tight to my dreams,
Refusing to be swayed by the schemes.

~

And then one day, as the sun kissed the horizon's gleams,
I saw it, my moment, like a scene from a dream.
A sign of success, a glimmer of hope,
Like a diamond amidst the vast scope.

~

I stepped onto a boat, my heart dancing with joy,
My hard work finally paying its dues.
And as I sailed away, the wind caressed my face,
I couldn't help but taste victory's embrace.

~

But here's the twist, the surprise in disguise,
That will leave you wondering, with wide-open eyes.
What awaited me on that distant shore?
What secrets were hidden in the core?

~

The story doesn't end here my friend,
For life is a journey, with no definite end.
As I reached that shore, I realized with glee,
That the true essence of success lies in setting oneself free.

~

So, I took off my crown, let go of my dreams,
And ventured into the unknown, amidst whispers and screams.

~

For life is not about reaching a certain place,
But more about embracing the journey, with grace.

~

And now, here I stand, with a smile on my face,
No longer chasing dreams at a hectic pace.
I've learned that the truest success lies within,
In finding peace and loving your own skin.

~

So, my friend, as you read this tale,
Remember that life's worth is not measured by the sail.
It's about the lessons we learn, the experiences we share,
And the joy we find in the moments we dare.

~

For in the end, it's not about the destination,
But about the journey, with its twists and turns,
It's also about the life lessons we live and learn.

~

So go forth my friend, embrace life's grand scheme,
And let your dreams illuminate your every beam.

Washed by Grace

Time: 07:06
Date: 22/11/23

In a world where darkness loomed,
I found myself longing to be consumed.
Searching for something to change my life,
I turned towards a path of divine strife.

~

Curiosity sparked within my soul,
As I questioned if baptism could make me whole.
Did it hold the power to transform my being,
And open my eyes to a new way of seeing?

~

With hopeful anticipation, I entered the water's embrace,
Anxious yet eager, my heart began to race.
But as the waves enveloped me whole,
I experienced a sensation that touched my weary soul.

~

Instead of drowning, I discovered the prize,
A feeling of peace, like the sunrise in the skies.
My doubts and fears began to subside,
As I realized the power of this symbolic ride.

~

Now armed with the word, I took a stand,
To expose the evil lurking in the land.
From adults to children, every soul should know,
The goodness of God and how it can bestow.

~

The journey, my friend, is not for the weak,
Mistakes are made, humility we seek.
But in those moments, we find the way,
To kneel down and pray, in hope and in faith.

~

And so, my tale unfolds, from darkness to light,
A journey filled with struggles but also with might.
Did it change my world, that fateful day?
Oh yes, dear reader, in every single way.

~

But the story doesn't end here, my friend,

For it leaves you wondering, where does it truly ascend?
In the depths of your heart, the answer resides,
As you embark on your own spiritual tides.

The Illusion of Connection

Time: 07:32
Date: 22/11/23

In a world of pixels and pings,
Where connections are made by virtual strings,
I often find myself lost in the whirlpool of social media's things.

~

What a lot of people don't understand,
Is that behind the filters and glam,
Lies a dark reality hidden from view,
Where hearts break and minds are shamed.

~

A canvas so vast, where thoughts and dreams are laid bare,
I tread cautiously through this digital lair.
For social media, my dear friend, is a mirror that reflects both
Light and despair.

~

It's a place where pretense reigns supreme,
Where authenticity is often just a meme.

~

But amidst the chaos and pretense,
There lies a sinister side that makes no sense.
Grown adults sit down and mock,
Those battling leukaemia in a struggle against the clock.
Their fingers dancing on the keyboard,
Spelling "encyclopedia" wrong,
Oblivious to the pain they prolong.

~

Social media was meant to be a tapestry of love and kinship,
A place to share laughter and friendship.
Yet, it has become a breeding ground where negativity thrives,
Where compassion and empathy hardly survive.
In this virtual realm, we meet to fight, disregarding the impact
On innocent lives.

~

Children, their souls fragile and tender,
Fall prey to the shadows of a digital blender.
Extorted and exploited, their innocence lost,

Their spirits crushed by the emotional cost.
Love and care, once cherished virtues,
Are now discarded without a second thought,
In this realm of false realities,
Their light is snuffed out,
Their dreams distraught.

~

So, as I navigate this labyrinth of likes and shares,
I'm reminded of the souls who suffer, unaware.
Behind every post, every comment, and every trend,
There are battles fought, both outside and within.
Social media, a double-edged sword,
where facades are adorned, and true selves are ignored.

~

And as I bid farewell to this digital stage,
I'm left pondering on a world that seems to rage.
A world where humanity takes a backseat,
And the true essence of connection is discreet.

~

For what a lot of people don't understand,
About social media's misleading hand,
Is that it holds both power and despair,
Leaving us wondering if anyone truly cares.

Toxicity Unmasked

Time: 07:45
Date: 22/11/23

I've had my share of toxic ex's,
Thinking that their toxicity was where the flex is.
But little did I know, it's a dangerous game,
A cycle of destruction with no one to blame.

~

I remember the first time we met, His charming smile, I couldn't forget.
But behind those eyes, a darkness brewed, A toxic poison that slowly ensued.

~

As days turned to weeks, the signs appeared,
The anger, the control, the things I feared. I tried to reason, to make it alright,
But his anger only grew, day and night.

~

I'd hear the yelling, the slamming of doors,
A constant battle, a war that waged indoors.
I'd hide the bruises, the scars from his rage,
Praying for an escape from this toxic cage.

~

But love can blind, and hope can deceive,
I believed his promises, eager to believe.
He'd say he's sorry, that it'll never recur,
But deep down, I knew the truth would occur.

~

The nights were the worst, filled with dread,
I'd lie awake, trapped in my own head.
Wondering why I couldn't break free,
Why love had turned into a nightmare for me.

~

But one day, amidst the chaos and despair,
A moment of clarity, a voice in the air.
I realized I deserved a life of peace,
To break the cycle, to find release.

~
I gathered the courage to leave it all behind,
To escape the toxicity that had defined,
My existence, my worth, it was time to reclaim,
To break free from this toxic chain.

~
Now I stand here, a survivor in my own right,
No longer a victim of the endless fight.
But as I look back on the pain and the strain,
I wonder how many others still remain.

~
Women and men, trapped in toxic love,
Their lives consumed by anger, like a glove.
I want to tell them, to set themselves free,
That there's more to life than misery.

~
So let this be a warning, a tale to be told,
Toxicity destroys, leaving hearts cold.
Break the cycle, find your strength within,
Choose love and peace, let the healing begin.

~
For toxic ex's may come and go,
But self-love and freedom will always glow.
Remember, you're worth so much more,
Break the chains, let your spirit soar.

~
And as I move on, leaving the past behind,
I'm grateful for the lessons learned in kind.
For now, I stand strong, no longer in pain,
A survivor, ready to embrace life's gain.

~
But in the depths of my heart, I'll always wonder,
How many more are trapped in this toxic thunder?
May they find the courage to break free,
To find love and happiness, just like me.

Echoes of Your Absence

Date: 16/11/23
Time: 22:00

The pain of losing you ran deeper than any other,
My blood ran cold when I heard those words from your mother.

~

A shiver of cold dread crinkled down my spine,
As 'Shermaine went home,' echoed in the hollow chambers of my mind.

~

A tsunami of grief swept over me,
Unleashing a flood, I had long feared,
Hearts broken head gone, I couldn't see clear.

~

They said your body broke down, but I never saw it coming.
We had plans and dreams, places to go,
But look at me now, what am I becoming.

~

I ran from the memories,
From our shared dreams tainted with sorrow,
From the absence of your laughter that used to echo in the hollow.

~

From the nightly ghostly whispers,
That left me with a bitter taste,
To the cold side of the bed,
To seeing your beautiful face.

~

I yearned for closure,
for a solace to numb the sting,
A respite from the relentless torment,
that your departure would bring.

~

I sought refuge in solitude where the voices would cease to exist,
Where the echoes of our past would dwindle into a distant mist.

~

Yet, in the silence of the night, the voices grew louder,
The cries, the whispers, the echoes of our laughter,
A haunting symphony of our past, a ghostly reminder,
That death is always near, so always remember to BE kinder.

~
And so, I fought, every night, every day, every moment in between.
A battle against the memories, the pain, the agony unseen,
Every tear I shed, every silent scream,
Was a testament to our friendship, a broken dream.
~
Here I stand, wounded, yet alive.
A reminder of a love lost, of a spirit that will survive.
With your memory etched in my heart, I promise to thrive,
For in every end there is a beginning, and in every ruin, life will revive.

The Symphony of My Love

Time: 08:25
Date: 28/10/22

Baby, there's a realization that struck me - the experience of truly connecting with someone intimately, exploring every inch Of each other's bodies, finding solace in their embrace, and indulging in a night of passionate exploration through countless positions is something I've yet to encounter in my entire life.

~

An epiphany, one might say.
In all my years on this earth, I've never made love, not in its truest essence - one of tenderness and intimacy.

~

I imagined what it would be like to feel the soft press of lips against my skin, tracing the contour of my body as if it were the Most precious artifact ever discovered.

~

I can picture herself reciprocating, exploring the other's form with the same intimacy for someone of the same reverence.

~

I yearned to curl up in someone's embrace, a protective fortress Against the world, a safe haven where vulnerability is the only virtue required. Whispering words of love would serenade in My ear, accompanying the gentle rhythm of two hearts beating In perfect harmony.

~

The thought of surrendering to another in such an intimate Manner will make my body feel alive with anticipation. The idea Of sharing the delights of making love, of exploring the contours of passion and desire, was both exciting and daunting.

~

Every position known to mankind and the ones we would Discover together, executed in the span of a single night. It Would feel like an intimidating yet thrilling prospect.

~

Despite my anxiousness, there is a sense of calm that would Wash over me. It is the realization that such an experience, Profound in its intimacy, would forever remain etched in my soul.

~

I could just imagine one understanding me fully, but most
Importantly, understanding the orchestra of emotions that will
Play the symphony of my love.

Ethereal Aroma

Time: 12:17
Date: 28/10/23

I can smell you even when you're not around.
Your manly fragrance lingers in the air,
sending chills down my spine.
It takes me back to a time when we used to sip wine,
Lost in each other's embrace.

~

Sometimes, when someone passes by,
I catch a whiff of that familiar scent.
My heart skips a beat, and for a moment, I think it's you.
My eyes dart around, searching for your face in the crowd.
But alas, it's just a passing stranger, unaware of the memories
They've unknowingly stirred.

~

The smell of you in the morning,
The smell of you at night,
It doesn't matter what time of day it is.
Your scent always seems to find me,
wrapping me in a cloak of nostalgia.
It's as if you've left a piece of yourself behind, imprinted in the
Very air I breathe.

~

I find myself yearning for more,
Desperate to hold on to those fleeting moments of connection.
I close my eyes and inhale deeply,
Trying to capture the essence of your presence.
But it's elusive, slipping through my fingers like smoke,
Leaving me with an ache in my chest.

~

I wonder, do you even realize the effect you have on me?
How your scent has become a tether,
Binding me to a past that I can't let go of.
It's both a blessing and a curse,
This ability to feel you without your physical presence.

~

As time goes by, I've come to accept that I may never have you
In the way I desire.
But still, I hold on to your scent,
Like a secret treasure that only I know.

It's a reminder of what once was, and what could have been.

~

So, I continue to search for traces of you in the air,
hoping that one day, our paths will cross again.
Until then, I'll keep inhaling the aroma that carries your
essence, and let it transport me to a time when we were
Intertwined in passion and love.

~

For now, the smell of you remains a tantalizing mystery,
A lingering presence that keeps me hooked, and never leaving
me.

Time's Captive

Time: 04:36
Date: 18/11/23

In the hazy mist of a sleepless night,
I find myself gazing at the moon's soft light.
Thoughts of you, an unending chore,
Linger in my mind, haunting me to the core.

~

Days blend into nights, and I'm on my knees,
Searching for solace, begging for ease.
Your radiant smile, a memory I adore,
Now lost to me forevermore.

~

I don't talk, I don't smile the same,
I'm just a shadow, a flickering flame.
Life took a turn, inexplicably worsened,
Leaving me stranded, my spirit hardened.

~

Three long years, yet the void still persists,
Your laughter, your touch, all I've missed.
A ghost of you, my constant companion,
In my dreams, in every abandon.

~

The world spins on, unrelenting and bold,
But I'm trapped in time, my heart still holds.
Will I ever find peace, or just keep on wishing,
For a glimpse of you, in my reality's stitching?

~

As I lay in the silence, my thoughts drift away,
To a place where the past and present sway.
I wonder if you feel this persistent ache,
If you hear my whispers for goodness sake.

~

And so, I remain, lost in this reverie,
A soul tethered to a love that's free.
Life goes on, or so they say,
But I'm still here, yearning for yesterday.

Seeking Divine Guidance

Time: 05:36
Date: 19/11/23

Once, in the quiet warmth of a humble place,
My world rested on a tightrope's grace.
My heart echoed a lonely pace, and in the mirror,
I gazed at an unknown face.
Yet within me, a voice began to trace,
The divine goodness in life's embrace,
A whisper that echoed, "God loves you, and in time things
Will fall in place."

~

From the strength drawn from my deepest aches,
To the times when hope seemed nothing but fake,
His divine path, I was led to take.
As if plucked from a nightmare, wide awake,
I realized, His guidance was no mistake,
The pain I carried, for His love,
He'd take, no matter what, for His sake.

~

Tears shed in silence,
wounds that throbbed and bled,
The horrors of a misunderstood childhood,
Etched in my head.
Yet, even in the darkness,
His tender light was shed,
Until finally, I grasped the truth,
And of His goodness, I was fed.

~

For He was the only one who saw my real hue,
The only one who in my worst moments,
My worth, He knew.
From kneeling on rough stones,
Praying for a life's preview,
To stepping on the red carpet,
My dreams in my view,
His grace carried me through,
And that's something every soul must pursue.

~

Now, here I stand, a believer, firm and true,

telling you, yes you, that His goodness is the real hue.
From the days when my stomach growled, hunger, my
only clue, to the nights when doubts in my mind grew,
His love remained steady, like the morning dew.

~

He held me close when temptations grew strong,
whispering words of comfort, forming a soothing song.
I thought I was at my end, I thought I wasn't that strong,
yet in His arms, I found where I belong.
He healed my spirit, proved my fears wrong, and now,
oh now, His love is my life's theme song.

~

And so, I speak of His goodness, from dawn till dusk,
till the stars twinkle, till the nightfall's husk.
My journey from a lost soul, from an abandoned husk,
to the bright lights of Hollywood, in His glory, I bask.
And if you're wondering why, just take off your mask,
let your soul be bare, reach out and ask...

The Tapestry of Time

Time: 18:29
Date: 19/11/23

As I sit here, the memories flood back in waves,
The pain and hurt, like a relentless maze.
Your absence weighs heavy on my heart, It tears me apart.

~

The days turned into years, and still I grieve,
The thought of your smile, I can't conceive.
Learning to smile again, it felt so wrong,
Knowing you'll never join me, hell is where I belong.

~

I couldn't bring myself to dial your number,
The silence, the absence, it tore me asunder.
How I longed to see you, just once in a while,
But now, you're in God's hands,
And I'll never see your smile.

~

Your fashion, your skin, your laughter so bright,
I miss them dearly, day and night.
It's scary to think, I'll never see you again,
The ache in my heart, it never does wane.

~

I wonder if you're watching, from up above,
Do you see my pain, my undying love?
I smile through the tears, but it feels so wrong,
The guilt, the sorrow, it's where I belong.

~

The memories of you, they'll never fade,
In every smile, in every cascade.
I'll carry you with me, every single day,
Until we meet again, I'll find my way.

~

And as the tears fall, and the memories compile,
I carry your essence, mile after mile.
One day, the mystery will unravel, and I'll see,
If in that moment, you'll be waiting for me.

The Human Network

Time: 05:11
Date: 21/11/23

On this healing journey of mine,
I stumbled upon a world sublime,
Live apps, diverse and alive,
with colours blending in perfect rhyme.
White, Indian, Mexicans, and blacks,
all joining hands on this digital track,
A tapestry of cultures, a vibrant space,
Where differences blended with grace.

~

Intrigued, I delved deeper into this realm,
Where no contracts held me at the helm,
A place where the taxman couldn't tread,
freedom from burdens, a thought in my head.
But as I watched their every move, their lives unfolded
Before me, going with the groove.
Sex, drugs, and alcohol, they embraced with glee,
A world that clashed with what I believed to be.

~

Yet it held me captive, this digital domain,
Like a moth drawn to an alluring flame,
For there was something more, beyond the facade,
Something deeper, hidden and odd.
The unhappiness in people's eyes,
A silent plea to be recognized,
To have their stories heard and understood,
Through pain and laughter, the bad and good.

~

But as I observed, I began to see,
They were mere pawns, a pay master's decree.
Their tears and laughter, a calculated game,
Manipulated emotions, a twisted aim.
Who were these puppeteers, pulling the strings,
Controlling lives like heartless kings?
A web of deceit, an illusion grand,
A truth that slipped through my trembling hands.

~

And so, I withdrew from this captivating scene,
Questioning what it all could mean,
The lives I witnessed on my digital quest,
Left me pondering, feeling unrest.
For in this vast world, so interconnected,
The lines of reality can become dissected,
What is true and what is fake,
A blur that leaves me wide awake.

~

So, on this healing journey,
I wander still, seeking truth beyond what's revealed,
For the live apps and their colourful facade,
can't hide the pain and longing, so raw and hard.
And as I reflect on this digital tale,
A myriad of questions within me prevail,
Who controls the strings of our lives,
And to what extent can we truly thrive?

~

So here I am, left with curiosity's flame,
wondering if I'll ever truly know the game.
The healing journey continues, with lessons yet to learn,
As I navigate this world, curious and concerned.

Embodying the Light

Time: 16:08
Date: 23/11/23

In a world full of pain and sorrow,
Where beauty is a facade and happiness seems borrowed,
I found myself yearning for something new.
I longed for a glimmer of hope to guide me through.

~

They say beauty comes from within,
But society's pressure makes it difficult to believe in.
I looked around, and all I saw was a sea of blue,
People wearing masks, pretending their lives were true.

~

In this twisted reality, I came across a few,
Souls so pure, hearts shining like morning dew.
They seemed immune to the chaos outside,
Radiating kindness and love, like a tranquil tide.

~

I was curious about their secret,
Their ability to stay strong, amidst a world so wrong.
With hesitant steps, I approached one of them,
Hoping their wisdom would quench my thirst, my gem.

~

She smiled and gently said, "My dear, it's not always easy,
But there's a choice we make,
To let love guide us when our hearts ache.
We refuse to succumb to the darkness around,
And instead, sow seeds of love onto the ground."

~

With each passing day, I learned from these few,
Their kindness infectious, their actions true.
They didn't break others to elevate their view,
But instead, lifted others up, and watched them bloom.

~

As time went on, their light began to spread,
Like a wildfire, their love knew no bounds,
It wasn't just in their head.

People started to notice the change in the air,
And slowly, they too started to care.

~

But just when everything seemed perfect and bright,
A storm brewed, casting a shadow in our sight.
Doubts and fears started crawling in,
Threatening to break our newfound kin.

~

Yet, as the tempest raged on, those few souls faced it head-on,
Refusing to let their spirit be gone.

~

They fought with love, defying the storm,
Holding onto hope, keeping their hearts warm.

~

When the storm finally subsided, a revelation transpired,
For within the chaos, true beauty had emerged, untired.
The world had witnessed the power of love and unity, and it
Forever changed its perspective and scrutiny.

~

And so, I learned that beauty does come from within,
But it's not just about the surface, it's about the love we bring.
In a world so broken, it's up to me and you,
To be the few who make a difference, to change the world's hue.

~

Now, as you reflect on this tale I've shared,
May it inspire you to be the one who dared.
To spread kindness and love, no matter how small,
For in doing so, you'll change lives, standing tall.

~

And so, my friend, the story ends here,
But the impact it leaves will forever be clear.
Will you be one of the few who chooses to rise,
Lighting up the world with your own vibrant skies?

Tresses of Transformation

Time: 16:34
Date: 23/11/23

In a world where the length of your hair was a measure of your Being, I found myself a curious anomaly, quite keen on Intervening.

~

My hair, much like a woven tapestry,
Held secrets, tales, and battle scars,
Traces of yesteryears, scattered like notes within a jar.

~

Hair can be filled with so many memories,
A tangible record of my life's enemies.
Each strand told a unique tale, of sunshine days and stormy gales.

~

Walking around with the same look, every day, every year,
I began to question - is this continuity really necessary?
Does a sameness in appearance reflect a sameness within?
The world thought so, but I refused to buy in.
So, I set off on a journey, seeking remedies, not for a cure for Hair but a cure for perceptions.

~

Growing older, understanding deeper,
I realized the necessity of shearing my coiled threads.
It wasn't a sign of defeat but a symbol of growth instead.
With each snip, I let go of past regrets,
Let in new chances, new sunsets.
My hair wasn't a fortress to hide behind,
But a beacon, a testament to my own mind.

~

As the scissors' cold edge met my shoulder-length mane,
I felt an inexplicable surge of power, a lion unchained.
The transformation wasn't just physical, but a metamorphic Revolution, shaping my ideals, my values, my solution.

~

Many saw my bald head, a peculiar sight, their questioning eyes
Filled with confusion, even fright.

But, I wore my bare scalp like a crown,
A badge of honor, with my head held high,
I refused to look down.

~

My hair had once been my security blanket,
My veil of conformity.
But now, standing bold and bald,
I felt invincible, far from stormy.
I didn't care that I was different, that people could see.
I smiled to myself, content in my diversity.

~

So, I cut my hair off and signed the tranquility treaty.
Not to fit in or stand out but to break free, such was my decree.
My hair or lack thereof wasn't the key to my worth.
It's my strength, my character, my joys, my mirth.

~

And so, I stand before the world, bare and brave,
Offering a story that's perfectly graved.
My tale may end here, but the questions persist.
What does your hair hold? Dare you resist?
The exploration of self is a journey without end, hair or no hair,
The message we send is the only thing that should ever depend.

No More Swearing

Time: 16:52
Date: 23/11/2023

In the heart of my mourning,
I found the strength to cease cursing,
A yoke of years in cathartic confinement,
Only profanity was reverberating.
Once I bellowed it high, oblivious to who were reacting,
Yet, the time had come to embark on a journey of mental
Refracting.
~
Buried deep within me was an inferno of fury,
Sarcasm was my only garment wearing,
Unearthing a seed of deeper empathy was all it took to quieten
The roaring.
~
Some may dismiss it as trivial,
Or even as the common tongue we bleat,
Yet this cessation of expletives rendered me exquisitely unique.
Realizing it was more than just a mindset,
But a proclamation that I'm far from being weak,
To abnegate negativity was indeed a gift,
It was all in mastering the technique.
~
Such a transformation was a revelation,
Like discovering a new path,
Walked each day without the furrowed brows or the aftermath
Of wrath.
~
And as I strode, the world listened, to the silence that I wore,
No curses did I need to express my thoughts, no, not anymore.
~
The umbrella of silence became my shield,
My banner, and my code,
A silent vow of peace, within which my true strength showed.
I discovered the power of words,
And the stronger power of restraint,

While others rained down curses, I stood firm, the silent saint.

~

As days turned into weeks, a change became quite clear,
Without the veil of bitterness, I could see and feel and hear.
Each waking moment brought a vision,
So vivid, so pure and so bright,
A world devoid of harsh remarks, was indeed a beautiful sight.

~

Now as I stand, reflecting on the journey from where I arose,
A whisper of gratitude escapes my lips, for the path that I chose.
The power of silence, the strength in restraint, a lesson I shall
Forever keep.

~

For in the absence of a profane storm,
I found a peace so profound and deep.

Love in Different Tongues

Time: 05:24
Date: 24/11/23

Once upon an evening, as shadows grew long,
I embarked on a journey, where I truly belong.
In search of restoration, solace, and peace,
I found a love language, that granted release.

~

My love language was simple, pure and true,
It was food and flowers, in delicate hues.
The joy of a sandwich, modest and plain,
Soothed my heart, as rain would parch grain.

~

A bouquet of roses, fresh from the box,
Raised my spirits, as music does to flocks.
The radiant petals in hues of sunset and dawn,
Amid life's sorrows, became my balm.

~

Yet, I discerned a truth about myself,
Uncovered a book from my heart's shelf.
A lover of words, of praises and joy,
Less of contact, avoidant and coy.

~

Touches and hugs weren't my winning card,
They came to me, unbearably hard.
But words of affirmation, they were my might,
A beacon of love, my leading light.

~

Presenting gifts, receiving them too,
Was an art I relished, a joy anew.
Each gift a token, of memories spun,
A silent testament of battles won.

~

Thus, on this quest to find my healing,
I discovered a language, so revealing.
A tale of love told in food and flowers,
Affirmations and gifts, in the life's fleeting hours.

~

Oh reader, now you know my tale,

A melody played on life's grand scale.
Yet, I leave you wondering, pondering on this,
What's your love language, your path to bliss?

Love's Departure

Time: 05:58
Date: 24/11/23

In an empty kitchen at morning's light,
I found myself in a curious plight.
Wrapped up in a soliloquy, my voice echoed softly,
"I really like this guy."
It wasn't just a casual remark, it was an admission stark,
Into the abyss of a hopeless heart, a revelation ready to embark.

~

The love I bore for you seemed to dissolve,
like sugar in a cup, it began to evolve.
A transition, a journey I wasn't prepared to resolve.
An emotional tap I had checked out,
my feelings for you without a doubt,
had taken an unexpected route, a liberating feeling,
making its debut.

~

Your looks, your actions, once charming and true,
were no longer enchanting, in fact, they made me blue.
Your image, in my head, shaped anew,
a realization I could only construe.
For the first time in my life,
I saw you anew, not as a lover but something to eschew.

~

Oh, how life truly spins, a wondrous spectacle,
a parade of wins and sins.
It brought us back to where we begin,
a memory of our love, now wearing thin.
Once, your face, a sight to behold, now repulsive and bold,
It invoked an eerie feeling,
A dread crawling on my skin, cold.

~

A grimace took over, contorting your features,
your fat face was nothing but a shadow of past leisure's.
It was a sight quite grim, yet as I walked away,
I bore the biggest grin.
A sense of freedom came from within,
a chapter closed, a new one to begin.

And so, with a heavy heart, but a cheerful aura,
I stepped into tomorrow's drama.
Wondering about the next panorama,
This story ended with a dash of melodrama.

Finding the Balance

Time: 22:32
Date: 26/11/23

In the depths of the night, under a sky so dark,
I found myself pondering, unleashing a spark,
A curiosity gnawing, deep within my core,
About parents and their children, a tale to explore.

~

Parents, the guardians, the ones in control,
But should they be chasing their kids, I asked my soul,
For children didn't ask to be born, it's true,
Yet parents hold the power, deciding what to do.

~

When a child fails to pick up the phone, oh so dear,
Some parents, it seems, close their lids, I fear,
The connection severed, lost in the abyss,
Does it not matter, the love that once was bliss?

~

And if, God forbid, a child should pass away,
Do parents forget, as time moves on, day by day?
The pain and the loss, does it fade away,
Or lingers forever, in hearts that were once okay?

~

Age, they say, determines a child's fate,
In some cultures, before 18, it's too late,
Children lost and broken, never to be seen,
Their dreams shattered, like a broken machine.

~

But let us not forget, in this curious tale,
That children were once innocent, breathing life's gale,
From the very same ribs, they came to be,
A human being, laying in a crib, so carefree.

~

So, my dear reader, as this story unfolds,
I leave you with questions, mysteries untold,
Should parents chase after their children, you see,
Or set them free, like pigs, forgotten and lost at sea?

~

For it is in these ponderings, where truth awaits,
In the depths of our hearts, where compassion creates,
A world where children are cherished, loved, and adored,
Where they grow and thrive, like a song to be roared.

~

And as the story ends, perfectly unclear,
I hope it leaves you wondering, holding it dear,
The power of parents, the love they should give,
To ensure their children, a life worth to live.

The Enchanting World of Swans

Time: 23:40
Date: 26/11/23

In the silence of the dawn, by a quiet river's bend,
I found myself entranced, caught in a state of wonderment
Without end.

~

There, amidst the gentle ripples of the water,
Bathed in the soft glow of the morning sun,
Were divine creatures, their elegance and beauty rivalled by none.

~

Swans, pure and white, gliding with such grace,
They were an explosive spectacle in that peaceful space.
As I watched their dance, a ballet on nature's stage,
My heart raced with excitement, my emotions hard to gauge.
They moved with a magnetism, a charm so profoundly rare,
Every twirl, every spin, kept me anchored to my chair.

~

Their wings, wide and powerful, spread in an eclectic display,
Painting pictures of ethereal beauty, in shades of silver and grey.
They danced on the water's surface,
Their performance truly authentic,
Indeed, they appeared as deities, their beauty seismic, magnetic.

~

Their legs, slender and pristine,
Stirred the water into a lyrical ballet,
Causing anyone who passed by,
Even the youngest of children, to stay.
There was an enchanting allure in their synchronized sway,
Every flap, every ripple made the onlookers' worries fray.

~

Always spotted in pairs, a graceful duo in perfect harmony,
Their unity a timeless ballad of love, a sight for all to see.
Their connection so profound, it echoed through their soft coo,
A profound testament of love, far purer than what we knew.

~

They pirouetted and twirled, bathed in the golden hue,

Their shared rhythm a testimony, a love so deep and true.
Their performance was a silent sermon, a lesson for me and you,
A reminder of the magic that happened when two became one,
Just two.

~

As the sunset painted the sky with a spectrum of colours divine,
I left that river's bend with thoughts intertwining like a vine.
The swans' mesmerizing performance, their love so pure and True,

~

Left me with a lingering question, one for me and you,
Can we too, learn to dance in life's river, with a love as
Profound, as lasting and true?

~

And so, it became a silent quest, a pursuit of a love profound,
Ignited by the swans' ballet, in nature's theatre, on the hallowed Ground.

~

A quest to find that rhythm, that harmony, that divine bond,
Where love echoes in every moment,
Where every twirl spins a love beyond.

~

And as I paced into the night, leaving the river bend,
The whispers of the swans' dance echoed their message was a Gift heaven-sent.

~

"Love, as we do, with a rhythm divine,
For such is the dance of life, such is the sacred design."

The Strength in Softness

Time: 23:55
Date: 26/11/23

In an age where the cosmos and stars were just discovering their
Gleam, There was a time when I was able to embrace my inner
Queen.

~

It was all so new, like a scene from a distant dream,
Stepping into my feminine energy for the very first time, it seemed.

~

I met a man, as gallant as could be,
His touch gentle, his spirit wild and free.
Every moment with him was a memory my heart longed to store,
Each second more resplendent than the one before.
In his company the world faded into a whisper,
Forgotten lore, his presence was a symphony my soul simply
Adored.

~

He took me to a place of bliss,
A realm where worries disappeared into the abyss.
Never had I been so loved, so seen, so clearly, my strength in my
Slender build, he understood, so dearly.
With him, I was a woman, carefree and bright,
The world's chaos lost in the moonlight.

~

A sense of tranquility swept over me,
As I knew he was more than just a suitor, he was my knight.
He would fight any demon, chase away any fright,
Enveloping me in his arms, my fortress in the night.

~

No longer did I feel the sting of being distraught,
For with him, a sense of safety was caught.

~

Each day brought a new surprise, a bunch of flowers,
Their scent a sweet lullaby.

~

He was my protector, my partner, his love, my ultimate high.
With him, I was more than just a passerby,
I was the queen, and he was my ally.

~
All good things, they say, must come to an end,
And our story, too, had to bend.
Was it all real, or just a beautiful pretend?
The lines blurred, the reality began to descend.
Am I still that queen, or just an old folklore, I continue to send?
~
Yet, the memories persist, the love, the laughter, the stolen kiss.
In the silence of the night, it's him I miss.
A story that started with a spark, left me wondering in the dark,
Was it him I missed? Or the feeling of being in my feminine energy
Which I embarked?

When Every Soul Meets Its Boon

Time: 02:54
Date: 28/11/23

In the heart of a time, where my presence was mere fiction,
I found myself lost in Brixton,
a detour, an unintentional expedition.
Three years of my life, like a ghost, I'd been away,
Yet fate steered me wrong, led me astray.

~

Driving through the maze, a sight caught my eye,
A body laid bare, under the open sky.
The scene hauntingly stark, replicating a divine conviction,
A life abruptly ended, bearing resemblances of a crucifixion.

~

Cloaked in a white blanket, as pure as untouched snow,
A young man rested, his face devoid of all glows.
His life, a tale untold, his journey abruptly paused,
His kin unaware, into a world of grief they would be tossed.

~

A handsome lad he was, yet he'd seen scant summers,
Little did they know, he'd danced his last numbers.
No ages he reached, his time was abruptly met,
A cruel twist of fate, his eternal debt.

~

Yet, his was not the only life that ceased,
Through my years of absence, the deaths had increased.
Splintered dreams, twisted tales of despair, not all in my mind,
Reality was daunting, to life's cruelty, we were all blind.

~

In sleep or wakefulness, the truth remained unturned,
Life's impermanence, a lesson harshly learned.
I've witnessed the end of journeys, tales getting their seals,
An observer in the shadows, documenting life's real reels.

~

And so, I drive on, through the echoes of these tales,
Guided by the moonlight, under the stars' trails.

Lost in the labyrinth of life, I continue my quest,
Haunted by memories, finding no rest.

~

In this life of ephemeral moments and fleeting dreams,
I am but a spectator, listening to the silenced screams.
Yet, the stories remain, buried deep within,
A constant reminder of life, love, and sin.

~

From Brixton to beyond, my journey is far from over,
Carrying tales of lives lived, like a seasoned rover.
Life has a way of spiraling, paths often deviate,
And in those unexpected detours, we meet our fate.

~

So, I ask you this, as I disappear into the night,
Are we the authors of our stories, or mere characters in sight?
As the sun rises, another day is set,
In this play of life, death is the only debt.

~

In the end, we're all stories, waiting for our turn,
A flame that burns bright, until it's time to return.
In the hush of the night, under the silent moon,
Life echoes in whispers, "Every soul meets its boon."

Embracing Solitude

Time: 03:36
Date: 28/11/23

In my quest to find peace,
I fell into my own place of being antisocial.
A longing for solitude and silence became my new goal.
No longer did I wish to engage in fights or be vocal.
I yearned for a life away from the chaos, away from the usual
Commotion of life's locals.

~

I decided to move away, far from the city's hustle and bustle.
The countryside beckoned, offering a chance to escape,
To live on my own terms, without the burden of being humans'
Garbage disposal.

~

The idea of seclusion held an allure,
A promise of serenity, and a respite from the constant social
Bombardment that had taken its toll.

~

And as I settled into this new way of life,
Something unexpected happened,
A realization dawned on me,
I discovered a profound appreciation for my own company,
The simple pleasure of solitude, and the freedom to create my
Own destiny.

~

No longer was I bound by the expectations of others or the
Constant need for validation,
I found solace in the silence, joy in the solitude,
And a sense of purpose in being my own custodian.

~

Yes, I fell in love with being on my own.
It became a sanctuary, a safe haven where I could escape the
Noise and chaos of the world,
And rediscover the essence of who I really was.

~

The love I once had for being around people faded, replaced by
A newfound understanding of the Beauty in becoming the
Unknown, the mystery of one's own existence.

~

As I sit here, writing this, I can't help but wonder about the
implications of this revelation.

~

Is it a form of self-discovery or the path to isolation?
Is it a temporary phase or a lifelong preference?
The answers elude me, leaving me curious and intrigued.

~

But one thing is certain: in my journey to find peace,
I stumbled upon a truth that has changed everything.
And I embrace this truth, embracing the enigma of my own
Solitude, and cherishing the beauty of Being on my own.

Eternal Sisterhood

Time: 04:12
Date: 28/11/23

In a realm where sunbeams connect the land and the sky,
Where whispers of wind carry memories high,
I search for your essence, a spectral figure,
With a heart alight, as profound as a river.

~

A star, maybe that's what you are,
Gazing from above, from a distance far.
Are you still chasing those radiant comets,
Getting high on moonlight sonnets?

~

Or perhaps, reading our earthly chats,
Smiling at the echo of our old, joyous laughs,
The silence lingers, making my heart shatter,
Against the spectral wind, your absence flutters.

~

Your absence, a sore echo in my soul,
A question asked with no parole.
Why, oh why, did you have to ascend,
leaving behind stories with no end?

~

Do you dine on nebulae in celestial banquets,
With an orchestra of stars playing sonnets?
Is it iciness of space that embraces you tight,
Or the warmth of eternity's soft, heavenly light?
Are you seated in the royal cosmic grandstand,
Witnessing the spectacle of your earthly band?

~

Looking down, do you see my strife?
The hustle and muscle, the love and life.
Do you see my tears and triumphs, see me succeeding,
Patting my back, in every meeting?
Your ethereal presence, a comfort, a blessing,
In each stride, you make me a queen.

~

Stay with me, dear sister, your love I host,
Even if you have become a spectral ghost.
In the rustling leaves, in the murmur of the sea,
In the sparkle of the stars, in you, I believe.

~

Though your mortal self has ascended high,
I know our love will never die.
From the cradle of the stars to the earthly dust,
In our memories and dreams, I'll forever trust.

~

Life and death, eternally merge,
And the spirit of sisterhood, forever emerge.

Rain's Magic

Time: 23:29
Date: 28/11/23

Even before my healing journey began,
I found solace in the rain,
Walking alone amidst the empty streets, feeling no pain.

~

With each drop that fell upon my face,
I let go of worries, a momentary embrace.
No need to think, no use for the brain,
I surrendered to nature's rhythm, free from strain.

~

The rain would beat against my skin,
And a newfound happiness would rise from within.
Unveiling emotions I didn't know I had,
A hidden joy, a feeling, so glad.

~

But one rainy day, something changed,
An unexpected encounter, my life rearranged.
As I strolled down a familiar pathway,
I saw a figure, lost and astray.

~

Curiosity tugged at my heartstrings,
As I approached, I noticed their fragile wings.
A wounded bird, soaked by the pouring rain,
In need of help, my compassion did sustain.

~

Carefully, I cradled the bird in my hands,
Feeling its heartbeat against my skin, life's delicate strands.
I sheltered it from the storm's relentless might,
Providing solace, a safe refuge from the night.

~

Together we walked, the bird and I,
Dark clouds above, yet hope refused to die.
With each step, a bond began to form,
A friendship born amidst the tempest's swarm.

~

Days turned into weeks, and weeks into years,
The bird once weak, now soared free from fears.

And as it took flight, leaving me behind,
I wondered what lessons I had yet to find.

~

For in the rain, where my journey began,
I found more than solace, more than just a plan.
A chance encounter had awoken my soul,
And now I longed for answers, a story untold.

~

So, I continued my walks in the rain,
Searching for meaning, a truth to gain.
For even though I had healed inside,
There were mysteries left to confide.

~

So, if you ever find yourself walking alone,
In the pouring rain, a melody of its own,
Listen closely, for the rain has much to say,
A tale that will leave you wondering, day after day.

The Metabolic Disadvantage

Time: 21:24
Date: 28/11/23

The glimmer of three summers past,
I, a beanstalk thin and fragile,
Embarked on a quest most curious and vast.
With dreams bloated bigger than my waistline,
I yearned to defy my metabolism's fast cast,
A war of wills and waist, a challenge unsurpassed.

~

Through goblets filled with cream and mountains of cake,
I'd dine in a gluttonous haze,
Surpassing the ravenous rat in his mealtime spate.
The scales refused to shift,
Their mockery slicing like a cold steel grate,
A daunting battle I was losing,
The grim, immutable hand of fate.

~

A glimmer of victory winked in the horizon,
When the taste of squid crossed my lips,
Oh, how it clung, and to my derriere gifted a slight tip.
The mirror mirrored a hint of newfound roundness, a prize
From my gastronomic trip.
Encouraged, I pledged an oath, a solemn vow not to quit.

~

A flight to Madrid, the land of tapas and sangria,
To taste their deep-fried pleasure, I'd yield to my food mania.
Surely, the lure of Iberico ham, croquetas, churros, would coax
My metabolism into a docile pet,
Tamed by Spanish gastronomy, I bet.

~

The fat, oh, how it conformed to my desires,
pooling in my eyes, tumbling down to my feet,
A sensation of completeness enveloped me, a moment so sweet,
A triumph, albeit fleeting, a momentary respite,
an incomplete feat.

~

For then, my metabolism, ever the defiant beast,

Roared its dissent, "No more meat!"
It decreed, its resistance renewed, its rebellion unleashed.
My taste buds rebelled, craving the forbidden,
The succulent feast.

~

And thus, the cycle continues,
The scales steady, my dreams uneaten.
A plea to the weight gods, this isn't defeat,
Only a warrior temporarily beaten.
To this day, you will find me, in dining halls, in kitchens,
A gluttony driven creature, still continuing to eat.

~

This tale I relay, of culinary pursuits and metabolic duels,
Ends here yet carries on.
Feast or fast, thin or fat, the mystery of the end, remains locked
Within.

Unveiling the Truth

Time: 22:07
Date: 28/11/23

Once upon a time, in a land filled with filters and hashtags,
I remember a time when I used to lay around,
Didn't have a care in the world, never putting my phone down.
~
In this digital kingdom, I roamed aimlessly,
Scrolling through social media, full of curiosity.
People's lives seemed perfect, captured in a snap,
But little did I know, it was all just a trap.
~
I would stroll through social media without thinking,
Watching people fake their lives while drinking.
Their smiles so bright, their adventures so grand,
But deep down, I knew, it wasn't the life I planned.
~
Then one day, as the sun kissed my face,
I realized this facade was just a disgrace.
This virtual world had consumed my reality,
And I vowed to break free from its superficiality.
~
I decided to explore the depths of my own soul,
Discovering passions that made me whole.
I took a step back from the screens that controlled,
And embraced the freedom that my heart extolled.
~
I realized that what we see is often an illusion,
A filtered version of someone's chosen fusion.
Don't watch other people's lives, a lot of it is fake,
And don't try to be like anyone, that is your biggest mistake.
~
Live for yourself, follow your own dreams,
For that's where true happiness gleams.
I set out on a journey, with no destination in sight,
Embracing the unknown, I spread my wings and took flight.
~
With each passing day, I discovered new heights,

Unveiling a world of wonder, beneath the pixelated lights.
No longer bound by the chains of comparison,
I soared through life, embracing my vision.

~

The beauty of being true to oneself, I realized,
Is far greater than any virtual disguise.
Live for yourself, not for other people's sake,
And in no time, you'll be flying like an eagle, wide awake.

~

And so, dear reader, as I end this poetic tale,
Remember to seek truth and let your spirit prevail.
For in a world where illusions often deceive,
Authenticity is what we must strive to believe.

~

Now, go forth and create your own story,
Leave behind the masks and embrace your glory.
And just like me, you'll find your own way,
I want you to keep wondering what lies beyond today.

Awakening the True Self

Time: 22:20
Date: 28/11/23

In a world full of betrayals and deception,
I rise like a Phoenix from my ashes.
Only against me, I'm back with vengeance,
ready to reclaim what is rightfully mine.
But my return is not merely a coincidence;
it is a calculated move to rewrite my own destiny.

~

Please listen carefully, for this is not just a sentence.
With every setback and heartache,
I've grown stronger, wiser, and more resilient.
I have learned the true meaning of independence,
Recognizing that my worth is not defined by the opinions of others.
It is within me, waiting to be unveiled.

~

Like a diamond buried beneath layers of coal,
The beauty within me shines in all its magnificence.
No longer will I allow any negativity to cloud my path.
What others say or do is irrelevant, for I have discovered the power of self-belief.

~

With a newfound focus, I embark on a journey to success.
But I am not foolish,
I know that wealth cannot be achieved overnight,
It requires diligence, hard work, and unwavering determination.
So, I roll up my sleeves, ready to put in the necessary effort to create the life I deserve.

~

But as I rise, a question lingers in the hearts of those around me.
They wonder how I have transformed from a victim into a victor.

~

They question my motives; they doubt my authenticity.
Little do they know that hidden within my soul lies a secret,
A secret that fuels my every move.

~
For within the realm of gods and graves,
I have acquired a power that transcends ordinary comprehension.
I can see through the intentions of those who cross my path.
I can decipher their true motives, their hidden agendas.
With this knowledge, I navigate the treacherous waters of life,
Avoiding traps and pitfalls set by those who wish to see me fall.
~
As I dive deeper into the world of success, the mystery surrounding me grows. People are captivated by my journey, intrigued by my transformation. They watch from the sidelines, waiting for a slip, a crack in my armour. But I stand tall, my determination unwavering.
~
And so, my story continues,
A tale of resilience and resilience, of growth and triumph.
With every step, I leave behind a trail of curiosity,
A burning desire in the hearts of those who witness my forward march. What lies ahead? Where will this journey lead?
The answers remain locked within the depths of my soul,
Leaving the world wondering, waiting for the next chapter to unfold.

Mental Fitness

Time: 03:35
Date: 26/11/23

"Keeping my mind pure from negative things,
is something I had to learn from what it brings,"
I often whispered to the stars above,
Yearning for peace, like a homeward dove.

~

My nocturnal strolls turned into mental clean-ups,
Ridding my thoughts of negativity's hiccups.
One night, under the diamond-studded sky,
Emerged a revelation, making my spirit fly.

~

"I finally realized that negativity never wins,
As humans we are puppets attached to negativity strings,"
I mused aloud, my words danced in the air,
Vanishing into the void yet echoed everywhere.

~

The city, with its skyscrapers so high,
Reflected my thoughts under the full moon's sigh.
The stars sprinkled wisdom, my heart was a lure,
"Purifying our hearts is something that we need to ensure."

~

It wasn't easy, courage it required,
Maturity untouched by the world's mire,
"It takes a lot of courage, and you cannot be immature,
Laughing at people has no cure,"
Wisps of my realization painted the night,
As I walked under the city's hazy light.

~

The echoes of ridicule, the shards of scorn,
Only resulted in spirits reborn,
"It only breaks them down or turns them into entrepreneurs,"
I mused, my thoughts resonating with the city's murmurs.

~

But the journey of a thousand miles begins with a single step,
So I decided to rectify, where once I was inept.

"If we want to start somewhere, we have to stop breaking others down, let's lift each other up, fixing our crown,"
I pledged under the moon's gentle frown.

~

As the dawn painted the city in hues of wonder,
I walked back home, my mind no longer under the burden of negativity's thunder.
The city awoke, oblivious to my nocturnal ponder,
Yet, the essence of my walk, in my heart did it render.

~

Under the city's veil, a thought did I sow,
A seed that would slowly, yet surely grow.
And even as the city moved on, in its relentless pace,
My nightly strolls bore the mark of a gentle grace.

Building a Resilient Mind

Time: 23:22
Date: 28/11/23

As I was living my dreams, I got so obsessed,
Every waking day, I would do my best,
A lot of it was filled with pain, but I know that was a test,
"I will be successful," is what I suggest.

~

It didn't matter how I looked, it didn't matter how I dressed,
I was not here to make others happy or to impress,
I was here to fight, to live my dreams,
To make sure that I will succeed.

~

So I continued to work hard and stay focused on the game,
Even if it meant I would go insane.

~

Days turned into weeks, and weeks into years,
I fought through the doubts and the fears.
Through sleepless nights and endless striving,
I pushed myself to keep on surviving.

~

But as the years went by, I began to wonder,
Was there something more to life, hidden under?
My obsession had consumed me, taken its toll,
I had lost sight of the bigger picture, the goal.

~

One day, in the midst of my frantic pursuit,
An old man approached me, looking astute.
He said, "Child, life's not just about success,
It's about finding joy and finding happiness."

~

His words struck a chord, deep within my soul,
I realized I had been chasing an empty hole.
Yes, I had achieved what I set out to do,
But at what cost? What did it all mean, and to who?

~

I took a step back, and I started to reflect,

On all the moments I missed, the people I neglect.
My obsession had blinded me from what truly mattered,
Relationships, love, moments that could have been treasured.

~

With newfound clarity, I leaned into the change,
I reevaluated my priorities, rearranged.
I still pursued success, but with a different lens,
One that valued balance and cherished friendships.

~

I achieved what I wanted, but at what price?
Were the sacrifices worth it? Was it all precise?
Now successful and accomplished, yet feeling incomplete,
Forever wondering if there was something I had missed, a beat.

~

And so my story continues, an ever-unfolding quest,
To find the answers to questions that won't rest.
For life is a journey, with no perfect end,
And it's up to us to determine what we'll defend.

Eternal Wanderer

Time: 23:43
Date: 28/11/23

For me, there was no better feeling than escaping the chaos and immersing myself in the tranquil embrace of the great outdoors.

~

With each step I took, a sense of liberation washed over me like a gentle breeze. The worries and stress of everyday life seemed to melt away, replaced by a profound sense of peace, It didn't matter if I was a doctor or a waiter – nature had a way of levelling the playing field, connecting us all in its majestic embrace.

~

As I strolled through the lush green forest, a symphony of colours unfolded before my eyes. The trees stood tall, their branches reaching towards the heavens, and the leaves whispered secrets in the wind. It was as if nature itself was inviting me to play, urging me to let go of the constraints of adulthood and revel in the simple joys of the moment.

~

I couldn't resist the allure any longer.
With childlike excitement, I picked up a fallen leaf and watched as it twirled in the air like a tiny dancer. The forest became my playground, and I was the happiest child alive. The world around me seemed to come alive, each tree whispering a different story, each rock holding a hidden treasure.

~

But amidst the wonder and enchantment, there was a lingering question in the back of my mind. How does this sense of freedom coexist with the realities of the world? How can we find balance between the beauty of nature and the demands of our daily lives?

~

As the sun began to set, casting a warm golden glow over the landscape, I reluctantly made my way back to the concrete jungle. But even as I returned to the city's embrace, I couldn't shake off the memories of my time in nature. The swirling colours of the trees, the sensation of freedom, and the joy of play lingered in my mind, leaving me yearning for more.

~

And so, the question remained unanswered, the mystery unsolved. How do we hold onto that feeling of liberation and connection even when surrounded by the daily grind? It was a question that fueled my curiosity, propelling me to seek the balance between nature's serenity and the demands of the modern world.

~

As the days turned into weeks and the weeks into months, I embarked on a quest to uncover the secret. I studied the works of great thinkers, sought the wisdom of ancient sages, and listened intently to the whispers of the wind. And slowly, but surely, the pieces of the puzzle began to fall into place.

~

Nature, I realized, was not just an escape. It was a teacher, a mentor, showing us how to find harmony in chaos. It whispered to us to slow down, to savour the simple moments, and to reconnect with the world around us. And through this deep connection, we could carry a piece of nature's magic within us, wherever we went.

~

So, armed with this newfound knowledge, I ventured back into the city, my heart filled with a renewed sense of purpose. The chaos no longer overwhelmed me, but rather served as a constant reminder to seek out the beauty and calm that nature had to offer.

~

And as I walked through the bustling streets, surrounded by concrete and noise, I couldn't help but smile. For I had discovered the secret, the missing piece that had left me wondering all along. Nature was not just a place to escape to; it was a state of mind, a way of being.

~

And so, dear reader, I leave you with this thought. Embrace nature, not just with your feet on the ground, but with your heart open to its wisdom. Let it guide you, inspire you, and fill your days with wonder. For in nature, there is no greater feeling, no greater teacher, and no greater mystery.

The Mirror Within

Time: 05:07
Date: 26/11/23

A world where ambition is a double-edged sword,
Where chasing dreams is both a burden and a reward.
I find it hard to give myself a break,
"I have to work harder, for goodness sake."

~

Once, a life that seemed riddled with blunders,
Where each stumble felt like being torn asunder.
Mistakes were my companions, they'd never forsake,
With each fall, my spirit, they'd painstakingly take.

~

There it was, the realization like a cascading river,
I had to change, had to become a giver.
The mistakes of the past were not for naught,
In their midst, a lesson hard bought.

~

Success and serenity, that was my new aim,
No longer a pawn in the world's relentless game.
Obsessed with the end goal, my vision never blind,
To become a better person, to always be kind.

~

I tread on a path, leaving behind familiar trails,
Old companions, mere memories in life's grand tales.
For realization dawned, not all who smile are friends,
And not all stories are destined to have amicable ends.

~

In the pursuit of greatness, this choice I made,
In God I trust, my fears began to fade.
The path of success was the manuscript I signed,
In the hope of a future, wonderfully designed.

~

Now I dance to the rhythm of my own beat,
Each success, each fall, a poetic feat.
In this journey of self-discovery and relentless grind,
It's my own identity, my own self, I hope to find.

Journey of the Soul

Time: 23:32
Date: 26/11/23

Heartaches meet fury, there was me, struck by calamity.
My dear sister, my best friend, was snatched away,
A wound time couldn't mend.

~

A burning question had me in its grip,
Why didn't you fight, why let it slip?
In the throes of my anger, I yelled at the skies,
Seeking answers to my whys.

~

In my mind, I saw you lay in that bed,
With God's whispers in your head.
Why did you listen, why did you give in?
His desires over mine, the ultimate sin.
There was a battle, but it wasn't fair,
My pleas unheard, my soul left bare.
In his celestial chessboard, you were the pawn,
He claimed the victory, and you were gone.

~

I often wondered about that eerie instance,
Your spirit's last residence.
What was your journey like,
As you left this sphere, did you hear us cry, our despair clear?
In your final moments, did you find peace,
Or were you lost in a crease?
Did a radiant light guide you on,
Or did our cries echo in your dawn?

~

The longing in my heart, a gaping hole,
Your absence, a merciless toll.
For one more day, what wouldn't I give,
One more moment for us to live.
But the universe decided otherwise, in this cosmic roll of dice.
You were taken away, not my choice to make,
Leaving memories in your wake.

~

Now I sit and pen this tale, my words a feeble attempt to unveil.
The sorrow and rage, the longing and pain,
A sister's loss, life's cruel bane.
Though you're gone, your echo remains,
A symphony forever etched in my veins.
I hope you're at peace in the cosmic beyond,
Your memory, my eternal bond.

~

And as my words culminate, I sit, I ponder, and I contemplate.
Was it destiny or a divine intervention,
That penned the climax of our relation.
In the grand scheme of the cosmos,
What is our place? Does love transcend time and space?

~

Perhaps, it's a mystery forever unsolved,
A puzzle intricately involved.
As I delve deeper, the answer eludes,
The universe, a labyrinth of platitude.

~

In this story of loss and love, of agony and the heavens above,
I find solace, even amidst the pain,
For in my heart, you will always remain.

~

This tale ends, leaving a lingering question,
A poignant reminder of our fleeting session.
In the cosmic dance of life and death,
What really matters with our last breath?
Peace, love, memories, or regret?
The delve in this mystery has only just set.

Ego's Grip

Time: 23:59
Date: 26/11/23

When love is fleeting and hearts often marred,
There was a man, arrogant, yet charming,
Who played the high card.
A multitude of virtues he did possess,
Yet a folly that undid all his best,
His stubborn pride that he'd never confess.

~

"It's a shame that we didn't make it to forever,
You were a good man a commendable endeavour,"
I mused, my heart heavy with tether.
He was a sight to behold, a captivating spectacle,
Yet his hubris overshadowed, creating a debacle.

~

His chiselled face and winsome smile,
Lured me to him, crossing many a mile.
But his prideful nature, as immovable as tile,
Ultimately led us to separate, experiencing our personal exile.
"You were a good man," I'd often whisper, "but not very clever."

~

Together we could've fought against the world,
Weathering the harsh and the swirled.
But his raging ego, tightly furled,
Ensured we were two entities, no longer twirled.
"I tried to fight for us, even through bad weather,
But your pride and ego made sure we were no longer together."

~

A man of forty-one, supposedly mature,
Yet allowed his emotions to obscure,
The love we held, so pure and sure.
His actions, a clear portraiture,
Of a man surrendered to his ego's lure.
"As a forty-one-year-old, you would think you've grown,
But you allowed your emotions to cover your own."

~

I stand today, in the memory lane of our love,

Looking at the sky above.
In search of a sign, a symbolic dove,
Hoping for a soul that fits like a glove.

~

"It's a shame that we didn't make it to forever,
There are better men who won't be stuck in their pride's however."
I sighed, a soft surrender, a declaration of hope,
A silent vow for an endeavour...
to find a love that lasts, a forever together.

~

The story lingers, a reminiscing echo,
A lesson imprinted from the man of ego.
It leaves one wondering, questioning the fiasco,
Will there be a 'forever' without pride's shadow?

Embracing the Warrior Within

Time: 01:49
Date: 27/11/23

The world around me spun, perched on a dizzying thread,
Seated in Surbiton, where daily my life bled.
Blinking lights met my blurry gaze,
In this town of timeless hue,
Days unfurled like film reels, the late nights too soon brew.

~

Afloat in the river of time, I felt the current, unmoored,
Life's soundtrack on a constant replay,
My existence ignored.
Not a ripple of purpose, not a wave of work to strive,
Adrift in my existence, was I even truly alive?

~

The tussle of bed sheets against the light of dawn,
The struggle to rise, to stretch, to yawn.
Yet, for Annaliese, I wrestled with the dread,
To put aside the enigma, of feeling better off dead.

~

The echo of these dark thoughts, never crossed my lips,
In the silent cacophony of my mind, they played out like movie clips.
My love for Annaliese was a salve, applying mends,
Yet the red haze of anger, clouded the lens.

~

I stumbled upon the snapshot of your memory, encased in a frame,
Lifeless, cold, and disconnected, I called out your name.
Yet, a sea of silence met my plea, deep and wide,
Why did you have to leave, and lay in the eternal tide?

~

The echo of my words, my poem's final trend,
Why did you leave? A question, leaving me at my wits end.

~
When your memory arises, my world is painted red,
A torrent of confusion, of questions that incessantly fed,
Why you lay motionless, why life from you had fled,
A riddle unsolved, a haunting symphony echoing in my head.

~
Through the labyrinth of my existence,
your memory, a constant thread,
Your absence, a gaping void,
your loss, a fate I endlessly dread,
Forever trapped in this limbo, an eternal homestead,
Between living and the dead, a chilling ballad of love and regret.

Unbreakable Mentality

Time: 02:25
Date: 17/11/23

His demeanour was placid,
His actions filled with rationality,
Yet his mind was an unsolved mystery,
A puzzle of perplexed actuality.
Day by day he persisted in his mundanity,
But the menace in his mind often questioned his capacity.

~

One day, the world shook with an unexpected calamity,
He was found in a sterile room of a hospital,
A victim of a merciless technicality.
The news travelled with a shocking velocity,
shattering my heart into shards of fragility.

~

A switch in his brain, they said, a twist in his neural plasticity.
His demeanour changed, shifting into an unfamiliarity,
I shuddered in fear, this was not his usual personality.
His eyes mirrored a different entity,
My love, was this your hidden duality?

~

His mind, a tumultuous sea caught in a storm of practicality,
oscillating between realms of realism and surreality.
"Where is the morality?"
I cried out in desperation, questioning the world's coldness
Towards mental health's gravity.

~

Yet, in the midst of this unnerving fatality,
My love for him remained an unbroken reality.
His split personality, a newfound characteristic added to his
Individuality.

~

I held his hand, whispering words of positivity,
Assuring him that this was our shared journey towards
adaptability.
His eyes, reflecting his simultaneous pain and vitality,
Bore into mine, acknowledging our unspoken confidentiality.

~

As I walked away from the sterile room's austerity,
A surge of resolve empowered my mentality.
The man I loved, still trapped in his mind's own city,

His strength and vulnerability my first love's ultimate
testimony.
~
In the end, however, some questions lingered with perplexity.
Was this his reality or an unforeseen abnormality?
The story of his suffering and my unwavering loyalty,
A tale of love, mental health, and echoing morality.

Heaven's Embrace

Time: 18:44
Date: 19/11/23

As I stand at the gates, I wonder what awaits,
Will I meet you here, at this heavenly state?
Your presence I long for, a smile on your face,
I can almost feel it, your warmth and grace.

~

I imagine you there, with curry goat on a plate,
We'll eat and we'll laugh as we reminisce and relate.
You always said I was greedy, my love for food so great,
But you cherished my cooking, it was our special trait.

~

Please, dear sister, don't let time abate,
Meet me at the gates, and let's celebrate.
We'll talk and we'll chill, in this afterlife's estate,
A reunion of souls, at heaven's grand gate.

~

As the days pass by, and the hour grows late,
I wait with longing, for our destined fate.
Will you appear, or is it left to debate?
The curiosity lingers, as I contemplate.

Positive Seeds

Time: 01:08
Date: 21/11/23

One breezy morning, as I walked down memory lane,
My twirling thoughts tied me in an ominous chain.
Life, oh life! It's a puzzle so strange,
A kaleidoscope of events, in constant change.

~

In the hustle of life and its rapid pace,
I forgot to live, lost in the rat race.
My soul was parched, my heart was hollow,
In the valley of superficiality, I chose to wallow.

~

Once, life was lush with positive seeds,
Now, it felt barren, devoid of deeds.
A chilling wind passed, whispering in my ear,
"Take a step back, let your needs be clear."

~

Overwhelmed, the reality had me stunned,
My spirit was battered, my energy was shunned.
It was time to focus; it was time to proceed,
A shift in mindset was what I indeed need.

~

Looking towards the horizon, with the future in sight,
I was ready to replant, to make things right.
To pluck out the toxicity, to let it bleed,
To plant again the seeds of positivity, indeed.

~

Under the silver moonlight, on a starry night,
I worked on my garden, with all my might.
I dug up negativity, watched it writhe and bleed,
I was determined to succeed, oh yes indeed.

~

Replanting positive seeds was no easy feat,
Had to be careful, as negativity was deceit.
But I moved forward, one step at a time,
Taming the chaos, I found my rhyme.

~

I watched them grow, these seeds of positivity,

In the face of storms, they showed their tenacity.
Life, oh life! It was no more a deceit,
It was a beautiful journey, sweet yet fleet.
~

Now as I look back, at the road I tread,
At the war with negativity, the words I said,
I found myself, in the midst of chaos and dread,
Replanting positive seeds, just as my inner voice led.
~

So, remember, dear reader, in the blink of an eye,
Life can mislead, make you fly high or cry.
But the power is yours, take the reign, don't cede,
Plant your garden with love, let positivity lead.

Personal Paradise

Time: 01:30
Date: 21/11/22

I asked God to help me with my dream home,
A place where I could truly be alone.
No need to ask Sandra, no need to ask Jerome,
For this was something I wanted to do on my own.

~

I didn't have to go out of my way,
Or travel to Rome to find where I'd stay.
A place of solitude, a place to call my own,
A sanctuary where my dreams would be sown.

~

The rooms were large, spacious and grand,
With floors that sparkled, like golden sand.
On my knees I'd pray, forever grateful,
For the blessings that came, without being hateful.

~

Now there were TVs, fridges, beds, and chairs,
Everything I needed, as if by magic, appeared.
No need to wait around, no need to check the bank,
For God had provided, without making me rank.

~

It just goes to show, if you believe in Him,
If you keep working hard, even when life feels grim,
He will see you through it, He will do it,
Even when you think there's no way to pursue it.

~

So keep the faith, keep pushing ahead,
Remember, you're not alone, there's nothing to dread.
For God's love knows no bounds, it's always near,
Just trust in Him and have no fear.

~

And as I sit in my dream home, so cozy and serene,
I can't help but wonder, what did this all really mean?
Was it my hard work, or simply His divine plan,
A mystery that leaves me in awe, unable to understand.

~

But one thing is certain, my dream came true,

And for that, I'm grateful, to God, I will always be true.
For He is the one who turned my dream into reality,
A testament to His grace, His love, His boundless generosity.

Life's Ruthless Tempest

Time: 01:56
Date: 21/11/23

In a town where time seemed to have stood still,
I dwelled, a victim of life's fickle will.
A tale of resilience is one to be spun,
A dance with destiny not easily won.

~

The sun smiled bright,
Coloured my world in a deceptive light.
I was a buoyant boat in life's vast sea,
Full of hope, as naive as one could be.

~

Little did I know,
The calm was but the calm before the storm,
The beginning of a journey that was far from the norm.

~

In the blink of an eye disaster struck,
Life rid me off my luck.
Like a merciless tornado, it tore through my existence,
Left behind destruction with no resistance.
An invisible shroud of agony had me smothered,
An echo of joy, now utterly unbothered.

~

Yet, life plays a sly game,
It never remains the same.
Amid the debris of my shattered reality,
A whisper of hope flickered in this tragic duality.
The portrait of despair was painted all over me,
But a defiant spirit refused to flee.

~

Each day, I dared to rise,
To look the harsh world in its eyes.
My shattered dreams, like scattered shards,
Reflecting rainbow hues under the starry guards.
Wealth or poverty, young or old,
Life spares none in its stranglehold.

~

It held me under, forced me to sink,

But through the turmoil, I began to think.
Amid the tumultuous tides and the chilling cold,
Emerged a tale of courage, waiting to be told.

~

Braving life's ruthless tempest, I found strength anew,
Learned to endure the worst, to pursue the view.
The pain, the tears, the relentless torment, were but trials,
Momentary segments.

~

In the depths of despair, I found might,
I swam ashore, into the light.
Life had torn me apart, indeed,
But I was not defeated, not conceding to the deed.
From the ruins of my past, I arose,
Marked by battles, yet radiantly composed.

~

And so, the tale remains untold,
The saga of a spirit uncontrolled.
The echoes of my journey still ring,
A testament to life's incessant swing.

~

For in the end, it's evident to see,
There's a savage beauty in life's unpredictable sea.
The story doesn't end here, but continues to unfold,
Etched in the annals of time, forever bold.

~

And here I stand, at the brink of the dawn,
wondering what the next chapter holds for me, thus drawn.

~

From the depths of despair to the heights of hope,
With life's tapestry, I continue to cope.
Each day a new verse, each night a new scroll,
In the epic saga of a resilient soul.

Unburdening the Soul

Time: 03:45
Date: 21/11/23

I found clarity,
Realized that everything is about consistency and parity.
Why would one love, if they lack steadfast ability?
A question that echoed in the halls of my tranquility.

~

Then you danced into my life,
Bringing chaos and toxicity,
Your cloud of masculine pride,
Disrupting my peaceful vicinity.
I was better off in solitude, away from your negativity,
Your presence was nothing but a challenging adversity.

~

Your desires, your wants, your hidden duality,
I walked away, left you alone, did it with public morality.
You wore your sexuality like a badge of audacity,
Yet, I bore no blame, no grudge, only a glimpse of pity.

~

Tears nurtured my strength, I moved on,
Wearing resilience as a crown,
But your audacious return,
Showcased a repeat of your well-known frown.
Same tricks, same games, same old familiar round,
The audacity of repetition, in your tunes I nearly drown.

~

So, I made my choice, an unwavering decree,
To forever leave you alone, to set my heart free.
I'd rather endure the storm now, embrace the agony,
Than live under a future of perpetual stormy sea.

~

As the sun set on our story, the pain felt like a shiver,
Yet, this tale of love and loss, leaves you in a wonder,
After all is said and done, I step into the river,
Of unknown, of new beginnings, of stories yet to discover.

Love's Symphony

Time: 03:59
Date: 21/11/23

There's a tale about love that I'd like to share,
A story so enchanting, it's beyond compare.
A tale that starts with a curious spark,
Lit in the heart, illuminating the dark.

~

"I simply love, love," I whisper to myself,
As I pull a tattered book from a dust-ridden shelf.
The book of my heart, bound in leathered emotion,
Swinging wildly between passion and devotion.

~

Love, my constant companion, more than a feeling,
Even when it leaves me in tears, staring at the ceiling.
It can be a tempest, a torrent, an unending tide,
Yet in its embrace, I find a place to hide.

~

There's a power in love, a strength untold,
Its magic is ancient, its story is old.
Love can be a balm, a salve, a potion,
But it demands of you, an unending devotion.

~

At times, it can sting, it can hurt, it can pain,
washing over you like an unexpected rain.
But those are the times it reveals its true form,
A storm that only in its passing, can transform.

~

The beauty of love, though, lies in its healing,
In the way it opens your heart, leaves you reeling.
When you find that perfect soul, it becomes a revealing,
A glimpse of a universe, infinitely appealing.

~

Love, it's a journey, a treacherous trek,
A game that even the bravest seldom play.
But when you find that special someone,
Who makes your heart sway,
You'd willingly kneel, come what may.

~
As I close the book, my tale of love ends,
Leaving a lingering curiosity, a question that sends,
A shiver down the spine, a quiver in the soul,
"What would be next? How would love play its role?"
~
A tale of love, as you've just heard,
Can't simply be confined to words.
It's a journey, a path, a road untraveled,
A riddle, a mystery waiting to be unravelled.
The recount may be over, my words may cease,
But love, ah love, it's a never-ending piece.

My Unforgotten Soul

Time: 04:39
Date: 21/11/23

In a forgotten graveyard,
Where the moonlight cast an eerie glow,
Stood a gravestone adorned with beauty,
Captivating all who'd come to know.
Its stone was polished with ebony black,
With golden accents bold,
An exquisite masterpiece,
A testament to a story yet untold.

~

Shermaine, your name etched in elegant script,
whispered secrets to the night,
Mystery and enchantment surrounded you,
Like a haze dimming the light.
I found myself drawn to your resting place,
Compelled to unravel your tale,
To understand the depths of your heart,
The emotions you failed to unveil.

~

Once, you were a vibrant soul,
With cheeks plump and rosy in their bloom,
Laughter echoed through the air,
Filling every corner of the room.
Your voice, a symphony in my headphones,
Reached deep into my soul,
Every word, every note,
A melody that made me feel whole.

~

But fate's cruel hand turned the tides,
And you were taken away too soon,
Now confined to this silent realm,
Where darkness casts its gloomy gloom.
Your spirit, once untamed and fierce,
Now lies dormant beneath the earth,
While you, my dear, are forced to witness a world devoid of mirth.

~
Oh, how I longed to keep you company,
To share in your joys and fears,
To witness your wrinkles deepen,
as the passing years turned to tears.
But life's tapestry is a tangled web, and time will only tell,
If our paths shall cross again, if together we shall dwell.
~

Shermaine, your gravestone stands proud,
a monument to memories past,
As I ponder the beauty of your life,
The moments that couldn't last.
And so, I walk away from your resting place,
With a heavy heart and a sigh,
Leaving you here in solitude,
As the moon bids the night goodbye.
~

But as I depart, a question remains,
A whisper in the night's embrace,
Will your story find its resolution,
Or forever linger in this desolate space?
And so, I leave you, dear Shermaine,
with the hope that one day we'll see,
A tale that unravels all your mysteries,
Setting your spirit forever free.

Love Yourself First

Time: 04:55
Date: 21/11/22

My heart, it danced to the rhythm of your touch,
But deep within, a doubt, I couldn't clutch.

~

For you, my love, brought me ecstasy untold,
Yet a strange feeling inside me did unfold.
It whispered thoughts of caution in my ear,
Telling me this path was not one to adhere.

~

Your identity, my dear, was abandonment,
Leaving me questioning your true intent.
And oh, your indulgence in food so sweet,
I couldn't help but worry, my heart's beat.

~

For it seemed, my love, you didn't love yourself,
A truth I observed, a truth I wished to delve.
Gently, I spoke, with utmost respect,
Urging you to focus on your own aspect.

~

But how could I, in love, ask this from you?
To change a part of you that made you true.
The battle raged within my soul's abyss,
For love and concern, entangled like a twisted twist.

~

And so, my dear, our story took a turn,
As love and doubts collided, hearts began to yearn.
Our chemistry, once strong, began to wane,
Leaving us both questioning and feeling pain.

~

The ending, my love, is one left unknown,
For our journey together has yet to be shown.
Will you find the strength to love yourself too?
Or will our love's destiny remain askew?

~

In this tale of love and uncertainty,

There lies a lesson, a truth for you and me.
That sometimes love can be both bliss and strife,
And it's up to us to find our own path in life.

In the Arms of Morpheus

Time: 01: 35
Date: 26/11/23

The dreams continued, but the fears disappeared,
A world of nightly visions that once had me ensnared.
Where nightmares were usual, now only dreams I revered,
An enigmatic domain of slumber, no longer weird.

~

Murmurs of existence - death, love, jobs, all unfeared,
They danced in my subconscious, in dreams they appeared.
The monsters I battled, the pleas that once teared,
Were but whispers in the echoes of dreams I once feared.

~

In some dreams, I was a fugitive, fleeing away,
From kin and companions who sought me in their play.
In others, I walked among glitz, under the spotlight's ray,
Marvelling at the rich and famous in their grand array.

~

The celebrity constellation - who were they really?
Were their dreams also spun in a tapestry so frilly?
Did they obey or command, in their reality,
Or were they marionettes in dreams, like you or me?

~

And then there were dreams, dark as coal and clay,
Where some unseen power demanded that I pay.
They coveted my soul, desired me as their prey,
Beckoning me to the devil's afterlife, where they wanted me to lay.

~

So, do tell, what are these dreams that won't sway?
Are they shadows of my reality or a mystical ballet?
Are they meant to guide, to warn, or merely portray
Fragments of an existence that has lost its way?

~

The dreams continue, the fears, they have gone astray,
And as for me, I ponder at the break of day.

In the symphony of life, are we but notes that play?
Or are we dreamers, forever lost in the cosmic grey?

~

And so, in the hush of night, I lay,
Awaiting the labyrinth called dreams where I wander and stray.
For in the end, aren't all of us but clay,
Destined to dream until we fade away?

~

So, I leave you to wonder, at my tale's sway,
Will you, dear reader, decipher the dreams' play?
Or will you, like I, be left puzzled at the break of day,
Forever questioning the dreams that refuse to obey?

Beyond Desire

Time: 03:56
Date: 19/11/23

In the realm of earthly desires, Amidst the wildfires,
I pledged a vow, puzzled you query how?
It was a commitment stark, in a world often dark,
I vowed to abstain, to liberate from physical chain.
No carnal dance, no lustful romance, in this game of life,
I chose a different stance.

~

Your curiosity piqued, you wonder what's next?
I found solace in prayer, yes, that complex text.
A relationship with God, intricate and profound,
In the silence of prayers, I found a holy ground.
Day by day, in baby steps,
I make my way, a path of faith, come what may.

~

Eyes on my career, I shifted my gear,
Planted seeds of positivity, fighting back the fear.
Entrepreneurial dreams in my head danced,
Businesses I managed, for success, I chanced.
I walked this road, hidden among life's codes,
A clear mind guiding me, shedding worldly loads.

~

Did I waver? Did I falter? Yes, I confess,
But perfection is a myth, in this worldly mess.
Blood still flows, the human in me shows.
The path was rugged, yet I didn't digress.

~

In this path, I stand tall, no diseases, no fall.
I live by the soul,
I've embraced that role.
I pray, I work, good deeds are my perk.
I choose to believe, in grace, I receive.

~

Am I perfect? Oh no, that's a hefty fee.
Simply striving each day, a better version of me to see.
Despite the trials, despite the pleas,
There's no way, no day, I'll catch those disease.

~
At the break of dawn, life continues on,
In the ink of the night, I pen this poem.
This path of mine, of love divine,
Will leave me wondering, at the finish line.

Through a Parent's Eyes

Time: 00:36
Date: 21/11/23

Once upon a time, in a world not so distant,
Lived young souls, gleaming, so persistent.
Whether they dreamt of goals on the green turf,
Or of crafting towers of architectural worth,
They stood united in their shared plight,
Yearning love and guidance, a future bright.

~

Through the lens of a parent, I share this tale,
A story of investment, where love doesn't fail.
Listen closely and you might glean,
The secret to raising kings and queens.
No matter their culture, no matter their ground,
It's overlooked often, yet it's profound.

~

Little Timmy, with twinkling eyes,
Dreamt of football and winning the grand prize.
His shoes were tattered and his journey seemed long.
Yet, with each clapped hand and supportive song,
We watched as he thrived, his confidence growing,
Love as his compass, his strength unknowing.

~

There was also Sally, a constructor at heart.
With blocks and bricks, she crafted art.
A silent support is what she craved,
A pillar of strength that steadied her pave.
With whispers of encouragement, and expressions of pride,
We watched as her creativity took flight worldwide.

~

Yet, children are delicate, like petals in the wind.
They're riddled with confusion, where do we begin?
To lie, to condemn, is to plant a seed,
That grows into a weed, chokes their creed.
Remove negativity from its root, not the stem,

Because as they grow, life will not be their playpen.
~
Here's the secret, the magic trick.
It's more profound than any magic stick.
Invest in your children with positive talks,
Instill in them courage, let them walk.
Let them stumble and fall, but be by their side,
With love as their shield, and truth as their guide.
~
This isn't a tale of mere fiction and rhyme,
But a testament to love's effect over time.
Will they achieve their dreams,
Become who they aspire?
This question lingers as the story transpires.
~
But one thing is certain, with love as their mentor,
Our children will inherit a world that's far better.
~
And now, I let this thought simmer,
As the lights of the day grow dimmer.
Have we done enough, did we get it right?
Are our children ready to take flight?
~
This story will continue, chapter by chapter,
On raising our future, the world's next actor.

Taking a Digital Detox

Time: 00:47
Date: 21/11/23

In a world consumed by screens and constant connectivity,
I felt the urge to escape and find some serenity.
The clamour of social media had begun to take its toll,
So, I embarked on a journey, seeking solace for my soul.

~

Leaving behind the noise, I ventured into the unknown,
Leaning on my inner strength, determined to be shown.
Away from my comfort zone, I sought a new chapter,
Ready to face the challenges, no matter how much I'd falter.

~

In the midst of my solitude, I felt a newfound clarity,
A chance to reflect, to discover the true me.
No longer burdened by the weight of the past,
I embraced the future, eager to make it last.

~

Through winding paths and untrodden trails,
I encountered moments that blew away past veils.
Nature whispered secrets that only I could hear,
As I shed old fears and embraced what was near.

~

With each step, I could sense myself growing,
Leaving behind the doubts and fears that were slowing.
A metamorphosis was happening within my soul,
Transforming my mindset, making me whole.

~

As days turned into weeks, and weeks into months,
I discovered strength I never knew I had in abundance.
The solitude became my haven, my source of rejuvenation,
A sanctuary where I could reshape my own foundation.

~

But as all stories have an end, my journey too had to close,
Leaving me with a bittersweet feeling that only time knows.
I returned to the world, changed and rearranged,
With a newfound perspective, ready to engage.

Now, when I hold my phone, I do it with intent,
Knowing that true connection lies beyond a comment.
I've learned to cherish moments, to live in the present,
For life's true beauty lies in the stories we create and represent.

Dying in My Dreams

Time: 01:01
Date: 26/11/23

That night I was plunged into darkness,
A surreal dance with death,
Gasping for my last breath,
And left pondering the profundity of every step I'd tread.

It had begun as a day of joy, of sunshine and laughter, an
Innocent picnic under an azure dome, where grass was green,
And joy was keen, besides me, life did roar and teem.

~

Laughter echoed in the air, innocent, pure and bright,
Every chuckle a testament to life's delight.
Try as I might, I could not cease my mirth,
The world was too radiant, too full of light.

~

But as dusk set in, a dark shadow loomed large.
His eyes met mine, a chilling encounter,
Tinged with a hint of danger.
And then it happened, sudden as a bolt from the blue,
I felt a shot, piercing through, lodged in my stomach, pain
Growing like rampant rue.

~

Running for my life, the pain was put aside,
Every corner, every turn, seemed to want my stride.
Walls seemed to close in, and stairs began to divide.
A surreal labyrinth, it felt, with the elusive safety of home, on
The other side.

~

My sanctuary, my haven appeared in sight.
But inside, it was a different plight.
My family was there, their faces a palette of shock and fright.
Yet only one cried, shedding tears that shone in the pale
Moonlight.

~

With every breath drawing thin,
I sought refuge in her soul within.
A prayer, whispered with my heart,

Tearing through the chaos, setting us apart.
"Just protect her forever, Lord, help her make the right accord."

~

She's just a child, yet to bloom,
Too soon to face an empty room.
She deserves love, she deserves pride,
Be her shield, be her guide.
I've strayed, I've erred, I've faltered in my stride,
But in her life, Lord, let no harm collide.

~

Floating away, into the night,
I reached out for the usual radiating light.
They speak of a tunnel, of peace, of warm embrace,
Yet all that unfurled was an endless space.
No pearly gates, no angel's chime,
Had I even made it to the other side in time?

~

My consciousness began to fade,
Slipping into an abyss unmade,
The symphony of medical devices played.
Tubes, wires and machinery in an orchestrated crusade.
The paramedics surrounding me, their expressions steeled,
Yet betrayed.

~

Thus, on this bewildering journey, I was suddenly apprised,
Of a cavernous darkness, where Hope and despair coexisted,
waiting to collide. In the face of death, what mattered were not
The tears shed, but the laughter shared, the picnic under the
Blue skies, the memory etched In the sands of time,
Where love and life itself reside.

~

And with that final thought, I closed my eyes,
Yielding to the unknown ride.
Would it mark the end, or a new beginning?
I was left wondering, as the world around me subsided.

Your Heavenly Adventure
Time: 02:38
Date: 26/11/23

I hadn't heard from you, my dear friend, in quite some time,
So I reached out with a text, a digital lifeline.
You were always my compass, guiding me through,
you knew what was best, in the gentlest hue.

~

But this time, your words were a puzzle, a mystifying index.
You said the situation was complex, a riddle, an unexpected reflex.
"When I get through this," you promised,
"I will tell you what's next."
I waited, my heart pulsating, my mind utterly perplexed.

~

The hours morphed into days,
And silence remained, no words were expressed,
My mind painted images, scenarios wild and grotesque.
Your silence was a symphony of concern, making me restless,
Until I received a message, turning my world into a tempest.

~

Your sister, with her words shrouded in distress,
Sent me a message of request.
With news of your health, my heart plummeted into my chest.
You were unwell, she revealed,
And my world convulsed under the weight of the context.
I felt a wrenching pain, my emotions convoluted and compressed.

~

Then came the call that left me breathless,
A video call that left my heart unprotected.
Your mother, her voice trembling, her face filled with regret,
showed me the image that I'll never forget.
Against the sterile canvas of the hospital bed,
your body laid bare, a tableau of threat.

~

Tubes and wires slithered over you, a mechanized network, a chilling silhouette.
I peered at the screen, my mind refusing to accept.
The vibrant friend I knew was now confined to that wretched bed.

This wasn't right, it was all so incorrect.
~
I sat there, my heart pounding,
My eyes stinging with unshed tears, my body in a state of neglect.
The story isn't over, this wasn't the end I had expect.
And so, I hold onto hope, to the promise of a better prospect.
I will keep waiting, for the day you resurrect,
From this terrifying ordeal, to the friend I recollect.
~
And so, we wait, for the dawn after the darkest night,
For you to emerge victorious in this fight.
Once again, the story isn't over,
It's just a pause, an interlude before you reclaim your might.
You said you'd tell me what's next when you get through this, and
I'll hold onto that promise tight.
For now, I keep my faith alight, waiting for the day you'll take that flight.

Purifying the Mind

Time: 03:35
Date: 26/11/23

I walked as an observer of human schemes.
Amidst the cacophony of life's mainstream,
My mind echoed with a peculiar theme.

~

"Keeping my mind pure from negative things,
Is something I had to learn from what it brings,"
I often whispered to the stars above,
Yearning for peace, like a homeward dove.

~

My nocturnal strolls turned into mental clean-ups,
Ridding my thoughts of negativity's hiccups.
One night, under the diamond-studded sky,
emerged a revelation, making my spirit fly.

~

"I finally realized that negativity never wins,
As humans we are puppets attached to negativity strings,"
I mused aloud, my words danced in the air,
Vanishing into the void yet echoed everywhere.

~

The city, with its skyscrapers so high,
Reflected my thoughts under the full moon's sigh.
The stars sprinkled wisdom, my heart was a lure,
"Purifying our hearts is something that we need to ensure."

~

It wasn't easy, courage it required,
Maturity untouched by the world's mire,
"It takes a lot of courage, and you cannot be immature,
Laughing at people has no cure,"
Wisps of my realization painted the night,
As I walked under the city's hazy light.

~

The echoes of ridicule, the shards of scorn,

Only resulted in spirits reborn,
"It only breaks them down or turns them into entrepreneurs,"
I mused, my thoughts resonating with the city's murmurs.
~
But the journey of a thousand miles begins with a single step,
So I decided to rectify, where once I was inept.
"If we want to start somewhere,
We have to stop breaking others down,
Let's lift each other up, fixing our crown,"
I pledged under the moon's gentle frown.

Replacing Love with Aspiration

Time: 03:47
Date: 26/11/23

I woke up with a rhyme at my lips, a song in my heart,
A tale of two souls - Chavanese and Ceecee, entwined by an
Oath, raddling the promise of a journey towards experience and growth.

~

"Listen, old friend, and lend me your ear,"
I sang to the mirror, my reflection echoing clear,
"We've travelled this far - you and I, together.
Reckoning the past, the future, and the in-between,
Through decades, through lifetimes, through spaces unseen."

~

In the silken, gossamer threads of time,
We've witnessed the throbs of hatred, the sobs of loathe,
Stinging, piercing, tarnishing our path.
Yet, we shall rise above,
For our souls are too resilient to buckle under their wrath.

~

My eyes, once lost in the dreams of love,
Now gaze upon the skyscrapers of ambition.
A future built brick-by-brick awaits,
A testament to unremitting dedication.
Love, let it linger at the rim of my reality.
Let it find me when I've charted my career's constellations,
When I'm touring the galaxies of success, devoid of hesitation.

~

This year, stained in the hues of focus and perseverance,
Shall bear the fruits of passion's resilience.
Distractions, like whispers of doubts, shall fall on deaf ears.
The future's a symphony in making, harmonized by dreams and ideas.

~

Oh, the day is not far when the spotlight will find my silhouette,
The applause would echo my name.

But today, in the quietude of my solitude,
I'll put my head down and see this journey through.
I'll nurture the ramparts of my dream,
Till they stand tall in the skyline,
A beacon burning bright and true.

~

And so, the story of life shall ink its own ending,
Leaving trails of wonder in its wake.
A tale of earnest yearnings, a saga of relentless churning.
A story spun around you, me, Chavanese, and Ceecee.
Silently, we scribe our lives, in the annals of time
And tell the story of our quest, unique, profound, and truly sublime.

The Borrowed Time Lifestyle

Time: 04:31
Date: 26/11/23

A click away from the information explosion,
I sit before my blinking screen,
Surrounded by a society that eludes serene.
My thoughts swathed in cascading rhythms,
Echoing, "We are on saving time,
Living in this day and age feels like a crime."

~

I was immersed in this modern world,
where the value of time has been inherently twirled.
Children birthing children, innocence stolen in a moment,
They are merely nine, but their childhood, they've spent.
Love and deceit have both been my intimate partners,
A dance under the digital spotlight, the essence of my prime quarters.

~

A culture of urgency engulfs our days,
Life's span seems curtailed in mysterious ways.
An invisible cage constrains our mind,
A paradox of liberation entwined with confined.

~

Yet, amidst the chaos, the stage calls my name.
I step forth from the shadows,
My destiny lies within the centre frame.
To party, to drink, was never a pleasure I sought.
I urge you to unshackle these bonds,
In awareness, you will be caught.
The chime of a notification, another email hits my inbox,
But I am master of my time,
No longer confined by the orthodox.

~

We are all living on borrowed ticks and tocks,
our lives intertwined within the grand cosmic clocks.
Thus, with every sunrise, I vow to embrace the divine,

I'll cherish each day as it unfolds, in this digital timeline, I will shine.

~

So, as my fingers dance on the keyboard,
Scripting narratives of digital lives,
I am reminded of our ephemeral existence, of our borrowed time.

The Phoenix Effect

Time: 04:51
Date: 26/11/23

A thirst for change began to kindle,
Sending sparks through my mundane routine,
My life, thus far.
~

A monotonous sonnet was set to take an exciting scene,
Over the next three years,
I wore my mind's resilience like a sheen,
Working hard for my goals,
Success was what I claimed.
~

I built an empire of words,
My fingers dancing on the keys,
Crafting compelling tales that were carried across the seven seas.
~

My reputation started weaving a magnetic aura,
Like the buzz around the bees,
The power within me, I realized
Was the potential I aimed to seize.
~

But beneath the sheen of my accomplishments,
There was a wound that time couldn't mend.
My heart yearned for someone I'd lost,
An irreplaceable friend.
Every night, under the obsidian sky, to the heavens,
A silent prayer I'd send, lamenting how after losing her,
In this life, I'd remained.
~

My heart ached for her presence,
Now lost among the stars,
Her laughter now just echoes,

Her memory a collage of scars.
Yet, I found solace knowing that above the skies,
Untamed, she danced in the heavens,
And for her happiness, I could not contain.

~

I decided to carve a new path,
Cast away the vestiges of my old hue.
I began to rise like a phoenix, resolute and true.
With each passing day, people began to review,
How much I had changed and grown, an inspiring view.

~

I understood that the world was for the flesh,
Not for spirits to accrue.
Life was but a fleeting journey, a temporary venue,
Yet I would keep working on himself until my time was due.

Guardian of the Skies

Time: 17:51
Date: 26/11/23

Bright as the brightest sunshine,
There was a bond that intertwine.
A relationship of the purest kind,
Like a precious gemstone hard to find.
Picture this: A love so surreal,
It filled the air with an ethereal appeal.

~

"I know you're my eye in the sky, "I would often mumble,
Feeling your presence,
Even when my world began to crumble.

~

The knowledge of your unseen gaze was ever so humbling,
An unassuming strength even when I was stumbling.

~

Sometimes, a strange excitement would consume my
heart, The idea of death, instead of causing dread,
Sparked a feeling akin to art.
For in death, I knew you'd be there waiting with your
Signature smile, A beacon of light across the celestial mile,
Enjoying a piece of divine pie,
The one with the cherries, as time continued to file.

~

Year after year, your spirit held me near.
In my darkest hours, your touch was clear.
A whisper on my skin, a soft, comforting din.
A presence so profound, in your love, I was found.

~

The thought of losing you,
Of you disappearing into the blue,
Filled my heart with dread anew.
But I clung to the hope, like a weathered yet sturdy rope,
That our bond would endure, true and pure.

~

"Keep watching over me, my spirit in the sky,"
I'd plea, eyes shut tight against the night's decree.
"Until the day we meet again, I'll embrace the joy, the pain.

Even though I know not when, on your eternal love, I depend."

The Shadows of Memory

Time: 18:25
Date: 26/11/23

Heartbeats and ticking clocks,
Where seconds morph into silent knocks,
I've learned a truth, both harsh and appealing,
No mortal can put a time on healing.
Aching hearts masked with glistening smiles,
Holding secrets, they bear for miles.
They carry burdens of which we know naught,
In the cobwebs of despair, they're often caught.

~

On the precipice of oblivion, some teeter,
Their final gaze towards ceilings, life's meter.
Bereft of hope, devoid of delight,
They wander aimlessly in the biting night.
Tread gently, dear ones, show compassion and care,
For you know not the weight others bear.
In this world of chaos, your kindness might be,
The beacon of hope for a soul at sea.

~

Look around, oh friend, and you shall see,
In every corner, humans dwell in melancholy.
Drowning sorrows in amber poison,
Seeking solace in its fatal liaison.
Veiling emotions, they soldier on,
Their silent cries echo till the break of dawn.

~

Haunted by specters from the innocent past,
Memories that were never meant to last.
Real-life tragedies played behind closed doors,
Etched deeply in hearts, forevermore.
Each scar a testament to the battles fought,
Each wrinkle, a chapter in the tale of thought.

~

We're all pilgrims on this journey of healing,
Daily battling unseen feelings.
Invisible wounds, bandaged by time,

Resonate within us, a melancholy chime.
Yet, amidst it all, shines resilience and faith,
A testament to the human spirit's wraith.
~

Our collected traumas, they do not define,
The limitless potential of the divine.
For we are not mere vessels of pain,
But phoenixes, rising from the ashes, once again.
And in this dance of healing and growth,
We find our strength, our hope, our oath.
~

So, let us tread softer, love deeper, be kind,
For we're all healing, in body and mind.
Let us hold close, the strength within us,
For the journey is long, and arduous.
~

And as the tale of our lives unfurl,
We'll realize, we're all pearls,
Formed by the grit of the world.
~

Forever in My Heart

Time: 01:46
Date: 28/11/23

In a world where certainty is rare,
A concept lingers in the air,
So frequently misused and misunderstood
"Closure", a word I devoured, with an aftertaste so sour.
I'm no broken heart pining to be heard,
Yet this grief I bear is no flighty bird.
It lingers in my soul, a relentless burn,
Even when the memories cease to return.

~

They preach the magic of time, its power to heal,
Yet such comforting tales bear no appeal.
The unyielding ache of a loved one lost to the bitter frost of death,
Renders life a heart-wrenching quest,
A challenge to draw another breath.
Here today, vanished tomorrow –
Their dreams and aspirations succumbing to sorrow.

~

Closure, they say, is the salve for the heart,
Yet what good is it when your world is torn apart?
I've chewed and mulled,
Swallowed and spat the bitter pill of this idea that's too hard to digest, I've learned instead, to adapt and adjust,
To live with the pain that has become a must.

~

My heart longs to see her again,
In a realm beyond earthly pain.
Until that day, my resolve remains,
Fuelled by love that never wanes.
This journey is far from smooth, the path is hard to thread,
But with her memory as my guide, I forge ahead.

~
A notion so profound, yet so absurd,
the quest for closure is a silent word.
Unseen, untouched, yet expected to heal,
the unseen scars that time can't steal.
The memories may fade, the pain may ease,
But closure is a myth, a mere tantalizing tease.
~

It's a struggle, an ongoing battle,
A fight that seems endless.
Yet, each day I face it,
Trying to make sense of this senseless.
But who's to say what the end will be?
With each passing day, the future is harder to see.

Resisting Temptation

Time: 02:06
Date: 28/11/23

Temptation lingers at every corner, I stood firm in my beliefs.
I never drink, I don't party, I don't smoke.
I'd rather find solace in the whispered melodies of nature,
The gentle rustling of the leaves,
And the soothing hum of the ocean waves.

~

While others sought for thrill and instant gratification,
I understood that life was not a joke.
It was a delicate tapestry of moments,
Woven together with purpose and intention.
It was a journey that required us to be awake,
To be mindful of the choices we made,
For we were not young forever. We had to stay woke.

~

Yes, I knew that our teenage years were meant for exploration,
For embracing the joys of youth.
But I couldn't help but observe my peers,
Going through life in a haze of smoke and blurred vision.
Everyday, they indulged in the greens that clouded their minds,
Numbing their senses and stealing away their dreams.

~

In the midst of it all,
I remembered that I was beautiful, inside and out.
And I needed a king, for I was a queen.
I understood that the path I chose was not an easy one,
But I held onto the belief that in due time,
My hard work would pay off.
And one day, when I had reached the pinnacle of success,
I would grace the big screens.

~

As the years passed, I watched my peers stumble and fall,
Their dreams slipping through their fingers like sand.
Their choices had consequences,

And they were left with regrets that haunted their sleepless nights.

~

But for me, a different story unfolded.
I immersed myself in books,
Expanding my knowledge and honing my skills.
I invested my time and energy in building a strong foundation for my future.
And as the world spun its endless cycle,
I found myself climbing the ladder of success,
One rung at a time.

~

The day finally arrived when my hard work paid off.
I stood on the big screens, not as a mere spectator,
But as a creator.
My words had the power to move mountains,
To inspire change, and to touch the hearts of millions.
I had become a storyteller,
A beacon of light in a world that often forgot its purpose.

~

As I basked in the glory of my achievements,
I couldn't help but wonder about the paths not taken.
What if I had succumbed to the allure of temporary pleasures?
What if I had lost myself in the fog of indulgence?

~

But as the curtain fell on my story,
I realized that everything happened for a reason.
My journey was unique, shaped by the choices I made and the values I held dear.
And in that realization, I found peace.
For I had stayed true to myself, guided by the belief that life was not a joke. I had stayed woke.

Manifesting Miracles

Time: 04:47
Date: 28/11/23

With a spark in my heart and a flutter in my chest,
I stand at the threshold of a brand-new quest.
A tale that has spanned over three arduous years,
A journey of triumph, doubts, and tears.

~

Once an apprentice, in the shadow of the wise,
I was just another dreamer in their eyes.
I sought so much, with such hunger and need,
Fuelled by a heart that dared to take the lead.

~

"Did I deserve it?"
I asked the flickering starlight,
My only company on many a sleepless night.
The answer, a whisper in the chilly evening breeze,
"It's not what you deserve, but what you seize."

~

Three years of relentless pursuit, not a moment of rest.
"Don't just dream, but manifest,"
I heard a voice say, sounding like a jest,
Yet, I toiled on, never ceasing, never repressed,
In my heart, I yearned for more. I was, indeed, obsessed.

~

Through days of sunshine and of storm,
Through every failure and reform,
I learned that a dream must withstand the test of time.
And so, I tailored my life to this paradigm.

~

Through the chapters of courage and the verses of faith,
I learned the rhythm of my dreams,
Their depth, and their weight.
For in the vast ocean of life's manifold mystery,
Each wave of possibility held a unique history.

~

Oh, what a journey the past three years have been!
I've wrestled with doubt, danced with joy,

And everything in between.
I've grown, I've healed, I've come to understand,
That life's greatest lessons often come hand in hand.
~
My dreams, they whisper, they sing, and they shout.
They light up my path, dispel any doubt.
"Be consistent," they tell me, "see all things through,"
For a dream is only as strong as the believer's virtue.
~
So here I stand, at the precipice of my dreams,
Ready to dive into life's flowing streams.
I've prepared so long for this moment, to be free,
To carve out the path that is destined for me.

Your Existence Will Cease

Time: 03:22
Date: 28/11/23

My world painted with hues of despair and agony,
Each day was a struggle, perpetuating its melancholy.
I was rowing my boat in a sea of torment,
The waves of affliction never seemed to relent.
Yet, in the face of adversity, I chose not to lay the blame,
For in the furnace of troubles, was growing my fame.

~

Then entered you, draped in the illusion of solace.
Convinced I was, you were the panacea to my distress.
Alas! Your intention was never to heal, but to play a game,
Disrupting my peace, you were not the same.
You thrived in chaos while I strived for serenity,
Your mere presence was a manifestation of volatility.

~

The realization dawned; I was embroiled in a ceaseless pursuit.
Unbeknownst to me, my peace was the coveted loot.
My spirit was the battlefield of your insidious game,
But it was up to me to extinguish the flame.

~

I found strength in my struggles, courage amid my pain.
I realized, to protect my peace, I must release the chain.
I was neither to cower nor to be caught in your web of deceit,
Instead, I opted to retreat.

~

And that's when it happened, I ceased
I refrained, I let go, like a dandelion dispersing its seeds,
I allowed your memory to flow.
I was no longer your captive, no longer a part of your game.
In the midst of all the chaos, I found my claim to fame.

~

Now, I stand in the limelight, basking in my glory.
My heart brims with content, for I have written my own story.
I am a testament of resilience, a symbol of self-love.
I am a beacon of peace, a gift from above.

~
So, heed my words, let them resonate in the silence.
I won't let your games distort my resonance.
I am my sanctuary, my fortress of peace.
In my world, your existence will cease.

Never Settle

Time: 23:21
Date: 28/11/23

The road I walked upon was not an easy one,
For it was paved with countless obstacles and trials.
Yet, I knew deep down that each challenge was only a test,
Designed to push me closer to my ultimate goal.
And so, with unwavering determination, I declared to myself,
"I will be successful."

~

In this quest, I discovered that appearances held no sway over
My purpose. It didn't matter how well-dressed or well-groomed
I appeared to others. I wasn't here to please or impress them.
My sole focus was to fight for the realization of my dreams,
Ensuring that I would triumph in the end.

~

The line between sanity and madness blurred,
But I refused to let it consume me.
For even when the world around me seemed chaotic,
I remained steadfast in my pursuit.

~

As I continued to work hard,
My focus on the game never faltered.
I knew that success was not a mere coincidence,
But a result of perseverance and dedication.
The burning desire within me kept me going,
Even when the path seemed impossible.

~

It requires resilience, sacrifice,
And an unwavering belief in oneself.
And if, perchance, you find yourself questioning the paths you
Tread,
Remember the tale of a dreamer who refused to settle for
Anything less than extraordinary.

The Bitter Taste of Envy

Time: 23:12
Date: 28/11/23

"Hear my story," I said aloud, my voice echoing across the
Crowd. The tale of a dreamer, once known as the crazy outlier,
Now basking in the fruits of choices that took me higher.

~

They said I was mad, lost in my dreams,
Too eager to swim against the torrential streams.
"You will fail," they would hiss, their lives mired in an abyss.
But I laughed in the face of their scorn,
For I knew the rose that bore the thorn.

~

Beneath the stars and along the city lights,
I saw the wealthy living right.
The naysayers gazed in disdain,
Their whispers harsh like pouring rain.
"Luxury is their game," they'd bark,
Their own paths shrouded in the dark.

~

Yet, I watched the wealthy not with envy in my eyes,
But as a student seeking the ultimate prize.
Studying their efforts, their minds, their way,
I began to pave my own pathway.
Now, in my grand abode, I lay,
No longer a spectator to the game others play.

~

"What's the matter?" I ask with a grin,
As their eyes dart from my face to my kin.
"Why does it matter where I dwell?
Why does my success cause you to repel?"
Their silence speaks volumes,
Their envy cloaked in gloom.
They don't understand the sweat, the toil,
How I turned dreams into fertile soil.
They don't see the nights of unwavering commitment

Or hear the echoes of my firm sentiment.
~

Their negativity I perceive,
Their jealousy I believe, is nothing but a deceptive weave.
It is the simple tale of those who choose not to strive,
Who let their dreams remain buried, never truly alive.
~

And so, I stand tall, my story echoing like a clarion call.
Hear me well, for this is true - I am living my dreams, what about you?
I've realized that one's joy lies in his own decree,
And negativity often stems from deep jealousy.

Writing a New Story

Time: 23:53
Date: 28/11/23

After three years, I am ready to close this chapter,
I am a human being, not an actor.
I've healed and I have learned from life's trials,
Now it's time for me to go the extra miles.

~

I am grateful to God for all that He's done,
But this time, I know that I have won.
I am thankful for everything I have overcome,
No regrets, for in my heart, there are none.

~

But amidst the triumph and newfound peace,
A curiosity stirs, refusing to cease.
For as I turn the page and bid farewell,
There's a story yet untold, a tale to dwell.

~

It begins with a dream, a flicker in my mind,
An idea that grows, leaving no room to hide.
A desire to create, to weave words and bring life,
To share my message, whether in calm or in strife.

~

I embark on a journey, armed with pen and paper,
Seeking inspiration, like an adventurous caper.
Through valleys of doubt and mountains of fear,
I push forward, determined to persevere.

~

With each word I write, the story takes shape,
Characters come alive, their voices escape.
They whisper in my ear, urging me on,
Their tales intertwined, forever to be drawn.

~

The plot thickens, twists and turns abound,
As I delve deeper, the mystery is profound.
Are you captivated, enthralled by the tale?
Each page turn brings both joy and travail.

~
But alas, as the story nears its end,
A clever twist awaits, around the bend.
For just as you think you may they know,
An unexpected revelation starts to show.

~
The ending is bittersweet, like a lingering sigh,
Leaving you wondering, questioning why.
A perfect closure, yet an open door,
A conclusion that leaves them craving more.

~
And so, my friends, as I bid you adieu,
Remember, every ending is a beginning too.
As I close this chapter, a new one begins,
With stories to tell, waiting for my pens.

~
For I am a writer, a creator, it's true,
And this is my journey, a tale for me and you.
So, join me as we embark on this ride,
In the world of words, where dreams coincide.

A Self-Discovery through Purposeful Games

Time: 02:22
Date: 27/11/23

It was a journey, through pebbles and flame,
A self-discovery, a purposeful game,
Three years I wandered in the wilderness of my soul,
Building bridges, filling an echoing hole.
Every day a step closer to the surface bright,
Guided by the stars, reflecting their light,
A healing process, painstakingly real,
Each morning, a little closer to the seal.

~

I chronicled the voyage in words spun with gold,
A hundred poems, courageously bold,
Each verse, a stitch on the tapestry of my heart,
Mending the pieces torn apart.
Written on the canvas of sorrow, yet gleaming with hope,
They were my lifelines, my survival rope.
A hundred healing hymns, each one a pearl,
My testament to the resilience of a girl.

~

Through stormy seas and calm spring days,
I danced with shadows and chased sunrays.
In every poem's rhythm, every rhyme,
I found strength, in my own time.
Oh, the lessons I've learned, the wisdom so deep,
From the heart-wrenching abyss, so steep.
Three years of healing, of growth, of rebirth,
I've found my footing, my place on earth.

~

Now a new dawn breaks, the past's veil lifts,
As the sea of time relentlessly drifts.
I've journeyed through darkness, embraced the light,
Learned to love the day and the night.
Three years, a hundred poems, a life renewed,
A soul that's resilient, a heart pursued.

I'm healing each day, but never fully healed,
A testament to a love that was strongly wielded.

~

In my heart's echo, I feel you near,
A whispering phantom, a memory dear.
Three years of losing you, three years to heal,
In every line, in every feel.

~

A tale that began with the loss of you,
Through three years and a hundred poems too,
It ends perfectly, leaving readers in wonder,
As I've found strength in love, in tear, in thunder.
And as you turn the last page, you'll finally see,
It's not just a story, but a journey through me.

Until it's my time, I will write.
With Love
Chavanese Wint

www.ingramcontent.com/pod-product-compliance
Lightning Source LLC
Chambersburg PA
CBHW070044230426
43661CB00005B/758